What's in it for YOU?

The author

"Ravi Mehrotra is a remarkable man. His life experience projects a rich tapestry of success achieved through sheer determination and hard work."

—The RT. HON. The Lord Dholakia, House of Lords, London

"Mr. Mehrotra is an inspiration to younger people and this book may help them to focus on what is important in this life and how best they can achieve their goals."

—Baroness Angela Harris, House of Lords, UK

"Mr. Mehrotra has shared his true life experiences which helped him gain wisdom to succeed in different and difficult phases of his life. His exhilarating journey, beginning just as a cadet (Marine Engineer) to becoming a Shipowner, unfolds the true spirit of an unbeaten entrepreneur."

—Mr. S. Hajara, Chairman & Managing Director,
The Shipping Corporation Of India Ltd.

"This book has something to give for everyone who reads it. It is also one of the few chances to receive insight into how someone can move from relative obscurity to being a successful and wealthy independent ship owner."

—Dr John M Doviak, Director, Cambridge Academy of Transport

"Ravi is a true ambassador of India's thoughts, traditions and, above all, entrepreneurship. His mantras for the success in life and business are simple, smart and, more importantly, straight from the heart. The book brilliantly brings out Sangam - that he is - of the two worlds - East and West! Read the book for a new dawn, a new awakening in your life !"

—Narendra Taneja, Journalist, commentator and thinker

".....makes inspiring reading both for the younger and older generation...."

—K. Venkataramanan, Member of the Board & President (O)
Larsen & Toubro Limited

What's in it for YOU?

Ten Lessons from Life
which helped me succeed

Ravi Kumar Mehrotra, CBE

First Published, 2012

MACMILLAN PUBLISHERS INDIA LTD
Delhi Bangalore Chennai Kolkata Mumbai
Ahmedabad Bhopal Chandigarh Coimbatore Cuttack
Guwahati Hubli Hyderabad Jaipur Lucknow Madurai
Nagpur Patna Pune Thiruvananthapuram Visakhapatnam
Companies and representatives throughout the world

Originally published by Amitabh Nagpal for Macmillan Publishers India Ltd
2/10, Ansari Road, Daryaganj, New Delhi 110 002

Original typesetting and page design: Arati Devasher, www.aratidevasher.com
Edited by Clive Birch MBE, www.clive.birch@booksbybaron.co.uk

Hardcover printed by Shree Maitrey Printech Pvt. Ltd
A-84, Sector 2, Noida (UP)

*"For my long time friends and mentors
Who have helped me to reach this
Pinnacle in my life"*

For the two most important women in my life:
my dear mother (the late) Amer Devi Mehrotra,
whose love and encouragement and wise words
have been my lifelong support and
my beloved wife Manju Mehrotra,
who has never for a single day doubted me or my abilities.

For my children
Saurabh and his wife Neha and
Manjari and her husband Utsav
and all my wonderful grandchildren.

To the new generation of achievers:
may you use the lessons in this book
and reach your own pinnacles of success.

All proceeds from the sale of this book will be
donated to the non-profit institution I have
established in my home town of Kanpur –
THE AMER MARITIME TRAINING ACADEMY.

Contents

FOREWORD BY SIR MARK TULLY   13

ACKNOWLEDGEMENTS   17

INTRODUCTION   19

RAVI'S FORMULA   21

RAVI'S TEN TIPS FOR RUNNING A BUSINESS   22

Life Lesson ONE
FAMILY FIRST   25

Life Lesson TWO
DREAM THE DREAM   37

Life Lesson THREE
MAKE YOUR MIND   45

Life Lesson FOUR
MEASURE YOUR TIME   57

Life Lesson FIVE
OPEN YOUR EYES   69

Life Lesson SIX
RISK IS RIGHT   75

Life Lesson SEVEN
FACE THE FIGHT   87

Life Lesson EIGHT
ESCAPE YOUR BOX   101

Life Lesson NINE
MAKE FAILURE WORK   121

Life Lesson TEN
ENJOY YOUR JOURNEY   141

Epilogue
IT'S NOT JUST ABOUT MONEY   151

Ravi's Ten Steps
ACHIEVING YOUR GOALS IN 40 DAYS   157

TESTIMONIALS   178

Foreword

by Sir Mark Tully

W e do tend to admire our opposites, those who do what we haven't done, perhaps can't do. That's why I have always admired men who have made their own lives, men of action, men like Ravi Mehrotra. I was in boarding schools all my childhood, where you were meant to learn independence, but I found myself being told what to do every minute of my waking day. After that I had two years in the Army, where I happily fitted into a routine which prevented me having to think for myself. From there to Cambridge, where life was much more ordered than it is today. Then finally there were two terms in a theological college, where I did find life too organised. So it wasn't until the ripe old age of twenty-four that I was told by my father there would be no more cossetting, and no more money so I'd better get out and find myself a job. Even then the job I found with the BBC was risk-free. It was so secure that on the first day I joined the Corporation my personnel officer said to me 'You may think it's clever to get into the BBC, but you will be a damn sight more clever if you ever get out'. So there I was back again, being cossetted by an institution so comfortable that I used to say working for it was rather like being a member of a club. At the end of my thirty years there I was presented with a pension for life. Perhaps, if I had been presented with Ravi's book when I was a teenager, my life might have been very different.

In *What's In it for You?* Ravi tells the story of his career and teaches us the lessons he has drawn from his experiences. He started as a naughty marine engineering cadet, was rusticated for ragging, went to sea and came ashore at a comparatively young age to have an adventurous corporate career in shipping. That included hazardous years in Iran before and after the Revolution. Ravi could well have continued as a corporate man but instead he took the gigantic risk of founding his own shipping company. There were times when he found himself sailing through choppy waters but he weathered the storms, expanded into other areas, and is now executive chairman of his Foresight Group. At the time of writing it has a total asset value of five hundred million dollars. What's more, as you can see from the cover, he's done all that with a smile on his face, a smile which I have never seen disappear.

From which of his lessons do I think I could have learnt the most? Perhaps it's his 'positive discontentment'. Ravi says 'remain positive but discontented with what you achieve, it will keep you aiming even higher, a sure way to keep the fire burning in your belly'. His discontent is positive because it is the opposite of the negative discontent of jealousy. So often people spoil their own successes by being jealous of those who seem to have achieved even more. For them the grass on the other side of the fence is always greener. They can always find someone who is richer than they are, or more famous. The renowned seventh century philosopher Spinoza once said that men, to judge by their actions, 'deemed riches and fame two of the highest goods'. The problem according to Spinoza was that 'men were never satisfied with them'. The Hindu law giver Manu said something similar: 'Desire is never satisfied by the enjoyment of the objects of desire; it grows more and more as does the fire to which fuel is added'. For Ravi 'wealth is a bonus, a byproduct of your journey, but not your goal'. He says 'Your true goal should be the enjoyment of the challenge and achieving your ambition. Therein lies true satisfaction'.

Ravi proved to be a talented engineer when he was a cadet. He showed remarkable talent as a manager when the Shipping Corporation of India transferred him from his ship to an office job. When he formed his own company he proved to be a talented entrepreneur. For all that, Ravi learnt you can't rely on talent alone. He tells his readers that hard work is also necessary if they are going to achieve lofty ambitions. Sadly many people think hard work means becoming a workaholic. They come to feel they are wasting valuable time if they are not working. But Ravi warns that work should only be one part of life and it has to be balanced with other equally important activities. He says 'Balance, plan, and enjoy your life. It is important that you weigh all your options in order to make choices that support a healthy and happy life for you and your family'.

Ravi realises that the happiness of any organisation for which you're responsible is important too. He says employees should be treated as members of a family. As a boss he makes sure he is approachable and social. That seems to me advice which is all too often ignored by modern managers and directors. When the cult of a very narrowly defined efficiency becomes too powerful, staff become units of production rather than invaluable assets. When the bottom line is all that matters, preserving the ethos of a company doesn't come into the reckoning. When management consultants become too influential, the voice of experience, people who know about shipping, steel-manufacturing, railways, or airlines will not be heard. What is called domain knowledge will be ignored.

Of course Ravi has not prospered by tolerating inefficiency, ignoring the bottom line, or being deaf to modern management theories. But the lesson I learn from him is that all these should be balanced with the need to run a happy organisation. In fact the need to find a balance seems to me to underlie all that Ravi has learnt. Balance your work and your recreation, and the time you spend with your family. Be prepared to take risks, but don't be foolhardy. Take the opportunities that come your way, but don't be for ever restless, looking for new opportunities. Don't get into a rut, but don't flit from job to job, as so many in today's corporate world do. Dream great things, but don't be unrealistic. Be positively discontent, but don't be eaten up by dissatisfaction – or jealousy. Seek success but remember you will probably have to face failure too. Here Ravi quotes Thomas Paine: 'I love the man that can smile in trouble, that can gather strength from distress and grow'. I am reminded of words from *If,* one of Rudyard Kipling's best known poems:

> If you can meet with triumph and disaster
> And treat those two imposters just the same ....
> Yours is the earth and everything that's in it,

And – which is more – you'll be a man, my son.

Chaturvedi Badrinath, a philosopher friend who taught me all I know about Indian thought, often reminded me of the importance of balance in Indian philosophy. In one of his books Badri wrote 'The question is one of knowing the true place of everything in the scheme of human life'. Badri went on with this warning: 'overvaluing any human attribute creates conflicts both within ourselves and with the rest of the world'. That seems to be a lesson that Ravi has learnt and it's not surprising because, although he is very much a citizen of the world and lives in London, he remains quintessentially Indian. Ravi himself says that, holding an Indian passport, retaining Indian citizenship, is sacrosanct for him and his wife Manju. When he decided to make a major contribution to those less fortunate than himself, he chose his home city of Kanpur in the North Indian state of Uttar Pradesh to establish the Amer Maritime Training Academy.

I have read this record of a very successful, but also wise man, with great profit to myself, and I should add enjoyment too. I am sure others who read it will find it equally profitable and enjoyable.

Acknowledgements

This book has benefited from discussions with many people over the time it has taken to write it. My thanks for sharing their memories and jogging mine go to my loving wife Manju Mehrotra; classmates and lifelong friends, my good friends Mr Upendra Misra and Mr BC Ganapathy for dredging up memories I had forgotten; my sister Mrs Shusheela Khanna, my sisters-in-law Mrs Bina Mehrotra and Mrs Sheely Mehrotra, and to Captain Yogesh Bhanti for the time he took to collect photographs and anecdotes from them; Captain D'Souza, Mr Amini, Amulya Mohapatra and others who went to great lengths to obtain photographs; close friends and benefactors Mr Paul Willcox and Ms Claire Horsley (who has also kindly read the proofs); Mr M Souri, Mr Ashis Basu, Mr Nezam Zeineddin and Captain Parampal Sidhu for their invaluable reminiscences; Mr Philip Newman of FotoFlite for allowing us to use their photographs; Mr Tom Leander for permitting us to reproduce articles from *Lloyd's List*; Foresight's staff and many others for their kind aid. I apologise to anyone I may have accidentally missed out, and shall surely include them in any future edition. Special thanks go to Mrs Parimal Chaudhuri for compiling the initial material and to Mrs Arati Devasher for her help in preparing the book for publication. I have referred to cities by their current names for the sake of consistency (for example Mumbai, which was earlier known as Bombay). As always, responsibility for any errors remains my own and they will be corrected in subsequent editions.

Introduction

'Mother-speak' can often be inaccurate, inadequate, replete with blunders or even unethical. But sometimes, if you are lucky enough, as I was, to have a mother like mine, you will find that all you ever wanted to know you have already learnt in her lap! And, quite literally, the nuggets of wisdom that she offered to me have served as tutor, philosopher and guide for most of my life. If you can make others see a benefit for themselves in something which is also in your own interests, you can win the world, as my mother Amer Devi Mehrotra, told me when I was really too young to understand the complete impact of that statement. And that's how the phrase 'What's in it for YOU?' originated – in my beloved mother's early sound-bites of wisdom, in those easy chats that a child often tends to neglect as 'motherly-blabber'.

My father, Professor C.L. Mehrotra, and my mother, Amer Devi Mehrotra, were both a part of the small, tightly knit and integrated community of Khatris (warrior caste or kshatriyas). Our branch is a spin-off from the larger Khatri enclave that belonged to the erstwhile Punjab of pre-independence India. However, for generations, we have resided in the northern-Indian state of Uttar Pradesh and so the majority of us do not speak Punjabi. My father, an academic, taught Economics at a local college; my mother and he raised a family of seven – five sons and two daughters.

My father was the architect of all my brothers' careers. Three of them studied to become medical doctors and one followed in my father's footsteps and became an economist. I was certain that I did not want my career to be decided for me, and that's one of the reasons I took up the hitherto unheard-of career (in my family) of becoming a marine engineer. Living in the landlocked city of Kanpur, the sea had never been a part of our consciousness. But to sea I wanted to go. It was an assurance that I would travel, see the world and expand my horizons beyond my hometown of Kanpur.

My life as a marine engineer took me into the big world out there across the seas, to explore new territories and ultimately propelled me towards becoming a ship owner. All through this long and exhilarating journey, that invaluable piece of 'mother-speak' kept replaying itself in my head and, later on, became the touchstone for almost everything I did. Experience is the best school, they say, but also the most expensive one. My simplest and toughest mantras, or Life Lessons as I call them, have had their genesis as I moved forward in life and age. There were some additional lessons that were learnt along the course of this journey, and they came to typify my own life.

The Life Lessons that I have gathered and the ones that have worked for me *en-route* are all offered here, illustrated by scenes from my own life. They are as much the story of my life as they are my saviours – because of them I regret nothing in my life. I hope, in all sincerity, that they redeem me as well as themselves as you share their genesis and fruition with me through these pages.

RAVI'S FORMULA

1. I realised from the start that family was the bedrock of everything I might do.
2. I developed a burning ambition to become a ship owner of repute within a specific time.
3. I discovered the whys of shipping after I had found the know-how of shipping expertise.
4. I worked out how to make time work for me, and how to time my work.
5. I learnt the importance of added value.
6. I taught myself to take a risk, to push the boundaries, to calculate the odds and fly.
7. I found out the hard way, when I faced disaster, that I must stand and fight.
8. I evolved a technique for remaining positively discontented with my own achievements.
9. I found the means to turn my mistakes to my own advantage.
10. I have let others decide whatever I have achieved, so they may speak for me.

Ravi's Ten Tips for Running a Business

1. Treat your employees as family – they will appreciate the concern and reciprocate the feeling and will also be more productive. With all the tension in the world, the best survival system is that of a family.

2. Always focus on the bigger picture. Never be complacent about what you achieve – aim ever higher and ensure that your deputies and employees know of your vision and have a clear idea of what you want them to achieve. Remain positive but discontented with what you achieve, it will keep you aiming ever higher, a sure way to keep the fire burning in your belly.

3. Knowledge is powerful and it is something to share and be shared. You can teach your people – they can teach you too. An enquiring mind never ages – for there is always something new to learn.

4. Keep the fire in your belly lit – by making a career out of doing the thing you enjoy most. Your subconscious mind will then work in tune and in time with your conscious mind and you will have a healthy urge to achieve more. As a sage once said, one plus one sometimes makes eleven.

5. When expanding or diversifying, open smaller branches elsewhere rather than enlarging the central office so that your expertise is never physically distant from the client or the target audience. It will also avoid the creation of empires within an empire in the central office. Use the opportunity to keep control.

6. If possible, avoid signing cheques yourself so that you don't look at the money as being your own, and you work for progress and achievement rather than monetary gain. As one of the Sufi saints I met in The Islamic Republic of Iran during the Iranian Revolution taught me, use your wealth as *amanat* (an Arabic word meaning 'financial trust'), as it will only beget more wealth and grow, not reduce. Trust is a risk you must take.

7. Be a benevolent figure. Be kind but demanding. Even when people disagree with most of what you are saying, their subconscious mind knows that you are trying to help, not hinder, and they will follow your guidance and, hence, progress. Don't fight them.

8. Work for your employees. Be approachable and sociable. Use the Japanese 'open office' system. Stop for sandwiches at lunchtime and chat together. Create a comfortable yet professional atmosphere in the workplace. It opens each individual's closed box.

9. Always profit from your mistakes, and those of your competitors within the same business, or outside it. And be forgiving – not to the point of folly, but as an act of generosity. After all, we all make mistakes.

10. Wealth is a bonus, a by-product of the journey, but not your goal. Your true goal should be the enjoyment of the challenge and achieving your ambition. Therein lies true satisfaction.

Life Lesson One

Family is important. Never undervalue it
or underestimate its contribution
to your success.

FAMILY FIRST

*The happiest moments of my life have been the few
which I have passed at home in the bosom of my family.*

Thomas Jefferson

One of the first life lessons I ever learned was that family is important. The familial relationship – whether by birth or by adoption – binds us and always requires more of us than we would give to anyone else. We are well rewarded for our sacrifices – they help us to better appreciate who we are. In our day-to-day interactions with our family we find out what and who we are and what is most important to us – our families hold the keys to understanding and appreciating ourselves. Who can relate better to us than our own brother or sister, who has shared so many experiences with us? Who can love us more selflessly than our own parents, who have sacrificed daily for so many years to raise us? The better we understand our parents and siblings the better we understand ourselves. Family is important because we are important and we need a group of loyal supporters. It matters what we think and feel and nobody cares more about us than the members of our families – at least, that's how it should be. Our family is there not only for our happiness, but for support in all aspects of life: for better or for worse, for richer or poorer, in sickness and in health – we need a family and that family needs us. When we support our families we will find ourselves supported in turn.

I began my life in India in the city of Kanpur, in the state of Uttar Pradesh, on 12 May 1941 (officially registered as 28 May 1943, the only time I needed that date was to fill forms in High School prior to taking examinations).

My father was Professor C.L. Mehrotra, who taught economics at the famous Vikramajit Singh Sanatan Dharma (VSSD) College in Kanpur and was the Dean of Economics at Agra University. My mother, Amer Devi, was a Sanskrit scholar, housewife and homemaker. It was my father's preference that she remained at home so all seven of us would benefit from her presence and, needless to say, to keep us all out of trouble and settle sibling squabbles. My mother was my heroine.

> I thought my mom's whole purpose was to be my mom.
> That's how she made me feel.
> Natasha Gregson Wagner

My mother gained my respect for many reasons, not least because she sacrificed a great deal for our wellbeing and to develop high ideals and good values in us. She instilled in me the conviction that I could achieve anything by sheer hard work. I followed this conviction throughout my career and still do today. It has proved to be the foundation of my success.

I recall a funny little habit of hers. When my brothers and I returned from school, all dirty and grimy, we immediately sat down to eat the lunch she had prepared for us, having washed only our hands and faces. Our mother would make fresh, hot *rotis* (Indian flatbread) for us. She, having bathed already and being of the old school of thought, was loathe to let our germs be transferred onto the *rotis* and the utensils she was using. So, she would seat us in a line some distance away from her, and toss us fresh *rotis* so she did not have to touch us 'unclean' kids! Hungry youngsters that we were, none of us ever missed a single catch!

> Our brothers and sisters are there with us from the dawn
> of our personal stories to the inevitable dusk.
> Susan Scarf Merrell

We were seven siblings, of whom I am the youngest, and my brother Murari Lal was the oldest. Bridging the twenty-year age gap between us were my sister Shushila, my brothers Shyam Behari and Bipin Behari, another sister – Kanti, and then my youngest brother Shashi Kumar. I remember many happy moments during my childhood.

My father would 'take tuitions' for the scions of the Singhania family, who were and still are an influential business family in India. In addition to his fee, he received bolts of greenish khaki cloth (which was material used for uniforms by the Indian Army) as a gift, on a fairly regular basis. This would be stitched into identical shorts for each of us younger boys. Though we found it monotonous, we were all aware of the financial circumstances of our family from an early age, and none of us ever complained about having to wear khaki garments all the time.

My brothers Bipin, Shashi and I shared a cupboard, in which each of us had a shelf – the top one was Bipin's, the middle one Shashi's, and the bottom one mine. We squabbled fairly frequently about mixed up clothing, but the bond between us was strong – we always made up and carried on as before, for my brothers were my best friends.

> *Family quarrels have a total bitterness unmatched by others.*
> *Yet it sometimes happens that they also have a kind of tang, a*
> *pleasantness beneath the unpleasantness, based on the tacit*
> *understanding that this is not for keeps; that any limb you climb*
> *out on will still be there later for you to climb back.*
> Mignon McLaughlin

Although we three youngest brothers were the best of friends, at times, like all siblings, we would squabble about something or other and shout at each other, each parroting what the others said over and over and over until we tired of it and made up.

I also recall that my mother used to call her three youngest sons and ask us to pluck out her white hairs! She always gave us a monetary reward, the size of which depended on the number of hairs each of us plucked! And if we wanted to eat ice-cream, which was considered a high treat in those days we would say that Shyam Kumari *bhabhiji* (sister-in-law), our eldest brother Murari Lal's wife, wanted to eat some. Our mother invariably allowed us to buy ice-cream when we used that excuse, and we would then be allowed some for ourselves too! All three of us were very fond of ice-cream, and it was my sister-in-law who paid for it!

I remember an incident from many years ago, when my eldest brother was married – it illustrates what regard my father had for his family and the special love he had for me. We were in Fatehgarh, where my sister-in-law to be Shyam Kumari's family lived, travelling from the train station to our lodgings in an *ikka* (horse-drawn cart).

Anyone who has travelled on one of these equipages will know that unless you keep a secure hold, you are liable to fall off as it jolts over the road. My *buaji* (father's sister) fell off the back and, as she rolled in the dust of the road, I yelled, 'Father! *Buaji* is dead! *Buaji* is dead!!' We quickly stopped and rescued her, and she was taken to hospital for treatment. Father was upset at having his beloved sister fall off, feeling that it was an insult to his honour as well as to her dignity. He would not eat any food for several days, and it was only when I begged him tearfully to eat that he did so, out of the love he bore for his youngest child.

We always ate dinner as a family, and then remained seated at the *chowki* (a low table in the kitchen) and continued to chat late into the night. Ours was a happy family and, in 1951, by the time I was ten years old, my eldest brother Murari Lal had married, passed his MBBS and was the only other earning member of the family apart from my father. My sister Shushila had married Mr Khanna in 1948. My brother Shyam Behari had by then begun a wholesale wood furnishings business. My sister Kanti was unmarried, and my next oldest brother Bipin was in the tenth grade. My fourth brother Shashi and I were still in junior school in Kanpur.

A happy family is but an earlier heaven.
John Bowring

It was at this stage of our lives that my father had a heart attack and passed away at the untimely age of fifty-one on 2 June 1951. His death had serious financial implications for our family – my mother had to provide for all of us with the exception of my eldest brother, Dr Murari Lal Mehrotra.

He who has gone, so we but cherish his memory, abides with us,
more potent, nay, more present than the living man.
Antoine de Saint-Exupery

Luckily for us, my father, the quintessential economist, had thoughtfully provided for his large family by building properties in Kanpur, using withdrawals from his pension fund. My mother was thus the thankful owner of two bungalows, which she rented out shortly after his death. We lived in a small portion of one of the bungalows – the house in which I had been born – and the rental income from both houses was the source of educational funding for five of us.

My mother just about managed to feed us and give us the necessary education – we even had to resort to stringent measures such as sitting in one room together to save the cost of electricity. Asking for anything extra was unheard of in our family. We were grateful for whatever we did have.

Naturally, I dedicated my first shipping venture to my mother, and she is the reason all of our ships have the prefix *Amer.* She spent ten months with me in London in 1986, and saw me become a ship owner in January of that year. She returned to India because the bitter winter was too cold for her, and shortly after her return, suffered a fall in the bath. My beloved mother passed away on 12 May 1987, a few months after her fall, at the age of eighty-three. I remember her each and every day.

The death of my father had also cut short whatever chance we younger boys had of going to an English-medium school. We remained enrolled in the Hindi-medium school next door, and in due course progressed to Vidya Mandir School for our senior school education. There the

Principal was Mangal Sen Bakshi and my most memorable classmates were Pradeep Gupta, Pradeep B. Kapoor, P.U. Satash and Shashi Kapoor.

It is such broad-minded mothers who are needed today. Good mothers are more essential than good wives.
Sri Sathya Sai Baba

Of the few toys or possessions I remember having in my childhood after my father's untimely death, one stands out in my memory. I was usually taken to and from school, and later college, riding pillion on my brother Shashi's bicycle. I hated this, and longed to possess a bike of my own, and not just an ordinary bike at that – I wanted a racing bike.

Our family's finances being what they were, I persuaded my mother that, if I graduated high school with excellent percentages, I would be given a racing bicycle. My mother agreed, putting a limit of a hundred rupees (around two US dollars at the present exchange rate, and twenty-one US dollars at the exchange rate at that time) on what she was willing to spend. When I passed all my exams with high marks, gaining a distinction in all my subjects barring Hindi and English, I began to look for a second-hand racing bicycle to purchase.

I persuaded one of my classmates to part with his bicycle for exactly the sum that my mother had intended to spend, having convinced him that his infinitely more well-to-do father (an executive in a textile mill) could afford to give him the latest model anyway. I took the greatest care of that, my first real possession, and kept it well maintained, well-greased and clean. When I eventually left to study at DMET in Kolkata, I sold it on again for the same one hundred rupees it had cost me, having kept it pristine throughout my ownership.

I look back on our family life in those faraway days, hard but happy times with my beloved siblings, and remember how close we were. In their different way, each of them left an indelible mark.

My eldest brother, Dr M.L. Mehrotra, became a deservedly celebrated doctor, entirely through hard work and his own merit, a leading specialist on tuberculosis, a member of the World Health

Organisation and Director General of the Tuberculosis Institute of Agra. He passed away on 8 February 2010. Of my other siblings, my sister Shushila, married in 1948, is over eighty years old and in good health. My brother Shyam Behari's wood-wholesale business did not do well because he was soft-hearted and could not collect his dues, so he closed it and then trained as a paramedic.

> To the outside world we all grow old. But not to brothers and
> sisters. We know each other as we always were. We know each
> other's hearts. We share private family jokes. We remember family
> feuds and secrets, family griefs and joys. We live outside the touch
> of time.
> Clara Ortega

My brother Bipin Behari began working with the Madhya Pradesh provincial government after his Masters in Economics; he was posted to Shivpuri, a hill station in the state of Madhya Pradesh, and we spent each summer there with him until 1960 when I went to the Directorate of Marine Engineering and Training in Kolkata. He subsequently joined me in 1986 to open my Delhi office as Director, Foresight India, and died in 1989 of heart failure at the untimely age of fifty-eight.

My sister Kanti, who married Dr Raj Kapoor in 1958, passed away in 1962, at the young age of twenty-seven, of a tubular pregnancy. My last brother Shashi Kumar, who was nearest to me in age, trained in medicine, passing his MBBS and MD with flying colours, and joined the Indian Railways Medical Services, before moving to a private practice as a general practitioner on the outskirts of Patna in Bihar. He joined me in Iran to work as a doctor with the National Iranian Oil Company in 1982, and then in 1989 came to oversee the Cyprus wing of my business until 1999, when he moved to my Delhi office, from which he retired in 2002.

Throughout my childhood, though we may have lacked material possessions, never once did I feel unloved or unwanted. When I needed help I received it. Love and affection were always given in full measure.

Encouragement in whatever we did was never lacking, and above all, family support was unstinting. My brothers and sisters and I have always been close, and those of us still here remain just the same today.

So it was that I learnt thrift from my father, care from my mother and sharing from my siblings – together we were and still are invincible, a true family.

Facing page: My father, CL Mehrotra

Right: A portrait of me in school

Below: My parents at a family wedding:
CL and Amer Devi Mehrotra

Above left: My sister-in-law Shyam Kumari and my younger sister Kanti

Right: My sisters, Shusheela and Kanti

Below left: My brothers Bipin and Shashi and I are grouped together at left, with my eldest brother Murari Lal to our left, with his wife Shyamlata in front of him. My sister Kanti is next to her, and my father is at far right. Also in the group are three of my eldest brother's friends from the World Health Organisation

Right: My eldest brother, Murari Lal Mehrotra and his wife Shyamlata

Life Lesson Two

Dream a little dream, then find
a way to make it grow.

DREAM THE DREAM

*Keep your dreams alive. Understand [that] to achieve anything requires
faith and belief in yourself, vision, hard work, determination, and
dedication. Remember all things are possible for those who believe.*

Gail Devers

Earl Nightingale's definition of the power of your thoughts is so accurate –
'We become what we think about most.' Your thoughts are always with you
and, repeating themselves in your brain, they encourage you either to take
action or to remain inactive. Listen to the voice in your mind Those thoughts
govern the success of relationships, whether personal or professional. They
illuminate the path to success. They always anticipate you and your actions.
Nightingale also said, 'The mind moves in the direction of our currently
dominant thoughts.' Dreams and even daydreams play an important role
in life, giving a vision of your future to inspire and motivate, or even a
goal towards which to plan. I believe that a person with great dreams can
achieve great things. If you don't dare to dream, you probably won't achieve
great things. Children are so often discouraged from dreaming, because
adults value logic and rationality above spirituality and creativity. Even
dictionaries describe a dreamer as someone who has big ideas which are
never realised. Tell others about your dreams and it won't take long before
someone criticises you for having ideas 'above your station'. But always
remember that, as it was for me, it takes just one dream to begin your
journey to success and happiness. Dream the dream, then live it.

My penchant for dreaming, my ambition and my drive to succeed did not blind me to reality, but instead led me to the realisation that lacking a mentor or 'godfather' who would hold my hand and help me to take those vital steps needed in life, I must make my own way. My thirst to achieve alone would be my guide. I remember that I was – and in my own right I still am – a compulsive dreamer. I also began to develop a hunger to rise above and beyond my father's achievements and my eldest brother's medical prowess.

The whole object of education is... to develop the mind. The mind should be a thing that works.
Sherwood Anderson

I continued in this vein, living a simple and uncomplicated life, until I completed my schooling at GNK Intermediate College (A levels) in 1957 where the Principal was H.L.Tandon and I learnt physics with two teachers – D.R. Arora and S. Damanji – while my namesake S.N. Mehrotra taught me chemistry and maths was in the capable hands of Dr Risheshwar Singh. Friends and classmates included Surinder Kapoor, Shambhu Nath, Birmani and Bimal Singhania.

In 1959, I passed my senior school examinations and began the first year of a two-year BSc degree at VSSD College, where my father had taught. It was at this point that I came across a prospectus for the Directorate of Marine Engineering and Training (DMET, renamed The Marine Engineering and Research Institute in 1994) in Kolkata, India. The College had been set up in 1947 to satisfy the growing need for marine engineers in India. At that time, this was the only such institute in Asia apart from those in Japan. Having looked through a prospectus wonderfully illustrated with photographs of cadets in white uniforms and a list of prospects and opportunities, becoming a merchant navy officer and having the opportunity to travel all over the world became intensely attractive to me. I decided then and there that I must make every effort to gain admission to this institute so that I could travel the world and ultimately realise my ambitions and find my own destiny.

Education is not preparation for life; education is life itself.
John Dewey

I appeared for the entrance examination of DMET in early 1960 and was lucky enough to be called for an interview. The panel of interviewers cross-examined me and then implied that I had enrolled at VSSD College for my BSc through the influence exerted by my father as a Professor there. I rejected this accusation and stated belligerently that my father had passed away nine years earlier, and the only reason I had enrolled in the course was because it was near my home and affordable. I was angry and annoyed by this – it was the first onslaught on my self-reliant status in the family and I told the interview panel very clearly that I was seventeen years old and did not need anyone's help to succeed – I was confident that I could survive purely on my own wits. They brought my interview to an end immediately and I was not sure I had made it but, as I was coming out of the door, I overheard one of the interviewers say that I was a suitable candidate for the merchant navy. I was secretly delighted and, confident that they would grant me admission, decided not to take the entrance examinations for any other engineering colleges.

Dreams are extremely important. You can't do it unless you imagine it.
George Lucas

I went back home and continued with my BSc course. At GNK Inter College the Principal was L.C. Tandon and the staff who helped me most were Ram Murti Dixit, who improved my maths, and B.S. Bhargav and G.D. Tewari, who kept me up to scratch in physics and chemistry.

To my great satisfaction, within two months of the interview I received a selection letter from DMET, commanding me to enrol in the session beginning in May 1960. It was to be a four year course in marine engineering and then a direct entry to a merchant ship as an engineering officer. At that time, India, under the Prime Ministerial capabilities of Pandit Nehru, was expanding India's merchant shipping, and the industry had a one hundred percent employment rate for marine engineering officers. Therefore, I felt on top of the world – I was sure that, upon graduating in four years' time, I would be assured a good job and would then be able to proceed on my way to achieving my ambitions.

My life was beginning to resemble a chessboard.

> *By playing at Chess then, we may learn: First: Foresight... Second: Circumspection... Third: Caution... And lastly, we learn by Chess the habit of not being discouraged by present bad appearances in the state of our affairs, the habit of hoping for a favourable chance, and that of persevering in the secrets of resources.*
> Benjamin Franklin

My father was a great lover of chess, and he had taught all his sons to play well. After his untimely death, my brothers Bipin, Shashi and I would play for seven or eight hours at a stretch, oblivious to all else. Our mother deemed it a distraction from our studies, and banned the game during the week, allowing us to play only on Sundays. Oddly enough, I compensated by using the skills that I had learnt from playing chess in my daily life. Whatever I did, I planned and strategised. My intuitive thinking was honed, and I treated even my daily chores like games of chess. This engendered self-reliance in me; soon, even though I was the youngest son, I gradually became responsible for helping my mother, running errands or doing odd jobs (a role known in Hindi as the *karta-dharta*). The skills I learnt while playing chess, and then honed by applying them to my daily life, have stood me in good stead to this day.

I had my dream, I had worked hard to make it possible, and now it was within my grasp.

Above: A portrait of me
during my college days

Facing page: GNK Inter
College in Kanpur

Above: VSSD College in Kanpur where I studied and my father taught

Life Lesson Three

Education is essential; an uninformed
mind can never achieve the goals
set by one's dreams.

MAKE YOUR MIND

*Life's up and downs provide windows of opportunity to
determine your values and goals – think of using all obstacles
as stepping stones to build the life you want.*

Marsha Sinetar PhD

To explain why education is important, I must go back to my undergraduate years, the grounding years of a professional's education, to remember my teachers, my subjects, the study and the play. Unlike many, I did not hate studying, but I have had friends who did not like the idea of studying beyond school. What was college life all about? It was, and indeed is, all about building on the foundation of our school education — it is where we gain the skills to soar high in life and enter the adult world in the pursuit of new dreams. Education gives us greater knowledge of the bigger world around us, develops a new perspective on life, offers like-minded friendships and builds opinions and points of view on everything. The conversion of information to knowledge and knowledge to wisdom is possible because of education. Education makes us capable of interpreting rightly the things perceived. Education is not about lessons in textbooks. It is about the lessons of life; it teaches us the right behaviour, good manners, how to lead our lives, and is instrumental in the development of our values and virtues. It turns us into mature individuals, capable of planning our futures and taking correct decisions, arms us with an insight to look at our lives and learn from every experience, to face life and to accept successes and failures, and forms a support system for talents to excel in life. Most significantly, it equips us with all that is needed to make our dreams come true. Education opens the doors to brilliant career opportunities. But education does not end there. It is a lifelong process. Self-learning begins at the point that marks the end of institutional education, though few of us realise it at the time.

I entered the portals of the Directorate of Marine Engineering and Training in July 1960. My mother managed to pay my tuition and hostel fees from the income provided by the rent from the properties my father had, fortunately, left her. My pocket expenses and the travel cost to the shipyard where I was apprenticed for the first three years of the course were funded by my stipend as an apprentice at the shipyard (this was a compulsory stint for all cadets).

My batch of cadets consisted of a total of one hundred boys, the maximum that DMET allowed per year, who ranged in age from seventeen to twenty-one. About sixty-seven cadets were based at the Kolkata campus and the remaining thirty-three were in Mumbai for the first three years, in order to take advantage of the shipyard apprenticeship facilities during the week, which were supplemented by evening classes; on Saturdays we had a march-past and a full day of classes. All one hundred of us then completed our practical training on boiler and generator sets and other mechanical apparatus in our fourth year at the Kolkata campus, which was used as the Head Office of DMET.

Innovation is the central issue in economic prosperity
Michael Porter

The shipyard where I was an apprentice for the first three years of my degree at DMET paid me an allowance of fifty-four rupees a month, but it cost more than two rupees per day to travel there, five days a week, and to pay for a meal in addition to the dry lunch supplied by the DMET hostel. I was, therefore, always short of money, as were many others. It was difficult for us to even have a night on the town in Kolkata, as we were permitted to do on Saturdays from four to eleven in the evening, and which cost us ten rupees at the very least. Innovative as always, we came up with a solution.

We would all gamble by playing *teen-patti* (a popular gambling card game played by North Indians especially before the festival of lights – Diwali) each Friday night and the winner would then have a gala night out. It enabled most of us to go out turn by turn – when we won. I did win fairly often, and admittedly it was a great high to the extent that I sometimes found it difficult to stop playing when I was on a winning streak. My great friend Upendra Misra and I made a pact that, since he never played *teen-patti*, he would take away my winnings when I had won enough for an enjoyable night out for both of us, and therefore stop me from playing any further than I should.

The strategy worked well, and we had quite a few memorable Saturday evening jaunts in Kolkata, and *teen-patti* is still one of my favourite games. I remember that it was during one of those jaunts that I visited a handloom fabrics shop to buy some white material for my mother. At the shop was a nice, helpful Bengali salesgirl who chatted me up, and the upshot was that we made plans to meet for tea later on. She was older than me by a few years, and we met several times thereafter in various tea houses and would go for walks and hold hands in parks and that sort of innocent fun, when I was in town on Saturdays. At the time, it seemed the height of romance, but our romantic relationship petered out a short while later, and I have not thought of that Bengali girl until now, raking up old memories.

At the time, most of us were away from our simple homes for the first time in our sheltered and unsophisticated lives, and had been educated in regional language schools. Suddenly, we found ourselves at a campus where we had to converse in English and eat bread with a knife and fork, instead of our usual *chapattis* (Indian flatbread), since we were engineer officers in training. We were also told that we must travel in first or second class railway coaches, and never in the lower classes, and were constantly 'ragged' by our seniors. To top that, we had to attend various marine repairing workshops allotted to us as apprentices, where we had to learn chiselling, forging, machining, fitting and overhauling of various items by assisting the workshop employees.

Of course, they took a sadistic pleasure in bossing the *babus* (a Bengali term meaning 'gentleman', used in this situation to imply insult) as they called us. Those of us who were Hindi-speaking were also promptly classified as Biharis (from the state of Bihar), who were generally despised in West Bengal, regardless of where we were from. You may well imagine our state of mind during the initial months at the campus; it was particularly difficult for those of us who were from relatively comfortable backgrounds, used to being pampered at home.

> *The ideal engineer is a composite. He is not a scientist, nor a mathematician, nor a sociologist, nor a writer, but he may use the knowledge of any or all of these disciplines in solving engineering problems.*
>
> N.W. Dougherty

As was, and indeed is, the norm at any professional institute it was traditional for senior cadets to rag new entrants to initiate them into professional college life. I was ragged a great deal, but learned to take it in my stride – I knew my goal was to see the world and I therefore never lost sight of that ambition. In addition, the purpose of all the ragging was to familiarise the students with their seniors so that a bond would be formed that would last all our lives and would be an asset in our future careers.

Ragging in those days usually commenced with a naked parade of all new students, while the seniors heaped abuses on their heads on the basis of their relative manhoods. However, they had a new prank to play... we were ordered to bring huge sheets of drawing paper and bottles of ink. The drawing paper was laid on the ground, our backsides smeared with ink, and we were enjoined to sit upon the paper. We were then told that the resulting 'artwork' must be framed and put on our cupboard doors in our hostel rooms... our first sight each morning would thus be both artful and innovative – that aspect of ourselves we could not normally see - and we had to bow to it before starting work.

In 1961, when I moved to the second year and the new batch of cadets came in, we followed the same tradition of ragging the new entrants. But things went woefully wrong – one of the students we ragged was related to the Governor of West Bengal. He tattled to the authorities, and four senior cadets, including me, were caught and rusticated. It was my first exposure to the power that can be arbitrarily wielded by those in authority. All my dreams were shattered and I ended up back in my hometown of Kanpur, where I rejoined the second year of my half-finished BSc at VSSD College.

The power of a thing or an act is in the meaning and the understanding.
Nicholas Black Elk

I was greatly upset by my rustication and tried every avenue to find a way to get back into DMET, but it was not until a fair amount of time had gone by that I found that one of my fellow expellees, a cadet called B.C. Ganapathy, who became a close friend, had connections in high places – he was a nephew of General Cariappa, the first Commander-in-Chief of the independent Indian Army and the hero of Western Command during the war between India and Pakistan. The General made a lot of 'noise' and the Government of India decided to reinstate all four expelled students. We lost three months in the fight and this period was considered by the Indian government as sufficient punishment.

Notwithstanding the heroes' welcome when we returned to college, and the nickname 'the four musketeers' awarded by our peers, the whole experience taught me a valuable lesson about taking risks and the consequences and repercussions that can rain down upon one. I could not afford to take any more risks with my career – I did not have anyone with connections and the resultant authority in my family to bail me out, and I never did so again. Instead I put my strategic skills to good use.

Titles are but nicknames, and every nickname is a title.
Thomas Paine

At DMET I developed a reputation for being a person who always had a plan or a strategy, and was most often successful in carrying it out. This derived from my fondness for chess and the skills I had developed by applying it to my personal life. Eventually, I gained a nickname that has stuck to this day – Guru. Though it was originally used by Upendra Misra, one of my close friends, gradually everyone began to use it, to the extent that some thought it was actually my real name, and later sent me letters addressed simply to Guru.

That nickname reminds me of a particular gameplan. Our final results at DMET comprised two sets of scores – from a written examination and from extra-curricular activities. I tried football and hockey but soon gave up, for there were better players than me. To compensate, I joined the DMET Marching Band as a bugler (not that I was much good at that either) and, in the final year, became Cadet Captain and scored high marks.

The one thing I could not do was learn to swim properly, since I panicked whenever my head went under water. Swimming carried a majority of the marks allotted for sports, and the test was taken at the Marine Club pool. This was presided over by the Junior Warden, Mr Mukherjee, who already held a good opinion of my friend Upendra, who had himself been an earlier Cadet Captain in charge of cadets lodged at the Club.

When it was my turn to swim, I got in the deep end, and was ready to swim to the shallow end. The moment the whistle was blown, Upendra engaged Mr Mukherjee in conversation, while two of my other friends joined them to block the master's view of the pool completely. Two more trusted cadets were deputed to hold my arms and tow me across the pool, joining the group around Mr Mukherjee when they were done! The moment they arrived, Upendra moved away and Mr Mukherjee saw me standing at the shallow end with everyone cheering me. I scored full marks. Nobody ever told tales and, if someone did go and rattle on the sly, neither Mr Mehta nor Mr Mukherjee took any action, though it was fairly common knowledge that I could not swim, and they were aware of my calibre in other areas. Since then, my swimming skills have improved and I now swim every weekend to maintain my constitution.

Necessity is the mother of invention, it is true, but its father is creativity, and knowledge is the midwife.
Jonathan Schattke

Another situation in which my innovative powers were required followed soon after the success of the swimming test, when I returned Upendra's favour. Our laboratory 'practicals' were due to be completed, and many of my friends absented themselves from these classes (taken in sessions of fifteen cadets) and copied the notes of those who did attend. Upendra was among the shirkers and, when examinations loomed, he panicked, suddenly realising that it was impossible to memorise all the procedures for every 'practical. The thought of failing made him queasy and he made my life miserable with his pleas of 'Guru! Think of some solution, Guru! Do something otherwise I may fail!'

I thought about it and came up with a plan. Taking an educated guess, based on the preceding years' examination papers, I managed to identify three of the professor's favourite questions as the ones most likely to feature in the examination and told Upendra to memorise those. In our favour was the fact that the professor and his laboratory assistant always piled up all the question papers at random on a desk, and examinees were called individually to extract one and then go to the relevant table already set up with the appropriate apparatus. We devised a fool-proof plan and all fifteen cadets in our session were induced to fall in with it.

Accordingly, on the day of the examination, each cadet pulled out a question from the stack on the professor's table, and 'read out' the name of the question he had memorised, regardless of what the question paper actually said. Having had the appropriate 'practical' noted against his name in the lab assistant's list, the cadet was to place the exam paper on the table that held the correct apparatus, and return to mill around with the other cadets. When all of us had been assigned our 'individual' questions in the same manner, all that remained was for each cadet to go to the station of the 'practical' which he had memorised – it did not matter what we had pulled in the first place! It worked like a charm, and each cadet neatly slipped into his place and completed his examination.

These exploits always required a great deal of guts, but that was one thing we were never short of! Our escapades were not confined to our studies. My friend Upendra and I got up to quite a few larks in our time... my 'romance' with the Bengali salesgirl had faded out, partly because a Kashmiri gentleman with a wife and two pretty daughters had been discovered living next door to DMET. Their mother was keen to find boys for them to marry; not Kashmiri like her husband, but 'eligible' boys with a good future (the merchant marine) from her own state of Uttar Pradesh. And there were the two of us ready and, to her mind, willing. We were invited to dinner, introduced to the daughters, and soon got into the habit of visiting their house fairly regularly – more, I am sorry to say, for the sake of the good food than desperation to marry the daughters!

They were lovely girls, cheerful and pleasant to talk to, and for the next eighteen months or so, Upendra and I went about in a blissful haze, full of good home-cooked food, pampered to the gills, and most definitely the objects of much envy among our peers. I was oblivious to the results of this prolonged interaction, but Upendra began waking up to the increasingly steely glint in their mother's eye and, with our graduation looming on the horizon, she was gearing up to lasso us! Upendra decided that we needed to make up our minds whether or not we were in for the long haul and, when he put it that way, my mind immediately jumped to the conversation we had had some time ago, when we had agreed that we would not marry until we had our Chief Engineer's licences and could take our wives aboard ship with us.

My skills of strategy and planning came into play once again. Putting my Guru cap on, I came up with the 'brilliant' idea of introducing two other equally eligible cadets to the girls, who did want to marry immediately after their graduation. It actually worked, to our incredulous surprise, and we were the objects of congratulations, having managed to 'transfer our responsibilities' to more willing shoulders. Many years later, one of those boys, who had joined SCI as a technical manager, was transferred to Tehran in Iran on deputation to Irano Hind Shipping when I was its Managing Director. He visited our home on the evening of his arrival and, while I was dithering about how to be tactful and considerate towards them in my introductions, promptly presented himself and his wife to my wife Manju as 'Guru's friend and ex-girlfriend'! Manju, thankfully, had already been regaled with stories of my various escapades and was unfazed and rather tickled by this event.

I worked hard after my return to college, and even had a technical paper – *The Hidden Advantages of Arc Welding over Riveting in Ship Building* – published in the Annual Magazine of the college in 1963. I then graduated in 1964, with an Extra First Class degree and as a candidate for the President's Gold Medal – which I was denied, because I had been rusticated and temporarily expelled in my second year, and that had tarnished my records. That was disappointing, but they did institute a new medal, of which I was the first recipient – *The Best All Round Cadet Most Suitable for Merchant Navy.*

Thus I completed my formal education, and added much to my personal learning – not least the knowledge that learning is a never-ending and essential process.

Above: DMET Institute Building

Below: One of the few
photographs I have of my days as
an apprentice at the shipyard in
Kolkata: (L to R) Arora, Mal and me

Above: Howrah Bridge was a landmark of Kolkata then and still is today

Left: When I began my career with SCI aboard ship

Right: Me at the start of my career

Life Lesson Four

Your personal life is as important as your professional one and hard work is essential for the success of both.

MEASURE YOUR TIME

Ambition is like love, impatient both of delays and rivals.

The Buddha

Edison's comment that 'opportunity is missed by most people because it is dressed in overalls, and it looks like work' is popular, and no statement could be more true. In my experience, people hope to get rich quick or to reach their goals by the easy path, and as soon as the path gets a little bumpy, they give up. It is important to work hard if you wish you achieve your goals in life. But if you commit yourself to working harder than everyone else you can achieve whatever you wish for – talent alone is not enough and there is no substitute for hard work. Differentiate yourself with hard work and knowledge or else you will be just another name in the pack, not to be celebrated and not worth promoting. To reach your goals, you must sacrifice certain aspects of your life – your family's support is essential for this. For most people, sacrifices are in the form of time. Create a life plan that satisfies all of your personal and professional aspirations, leaving quality time for your family, and fitting everything into a reasonable time schedule. I've always felt that, at the end of my life, if all I had to show for my hard work and hectic schedule was wealth, while my family never saw me, and my health suffered terribly because I drove myself too hard, I would have to ask myself 'Was it really worth it?' Balance, plan and enjoy your life. It is important that you weigh all your options in order to make choices that support a healthy and happy life for you and your family.

There were two shipping companies that I could have joined after graduating from DMET – the Scindia Steam Navigation Company which was the oldest company in India and the Shipping Corporation of India which had been created by the Government of India in 1962. Being young, and therefore eager to progress in my chosen profession, I chose the company that offered the quickest opportunity to achieve the rank of Chief Engineer, if I could pass the examination and get the requisite Chief Engineer's Licence – the Shipping Corporation of India (SCI). I joined SCI in 1964, sailed as a marine engineer on their ships and saw the world. My first dream was fulfilled, only to lead on to greater dreams fuelled by my ambition, which was greater than ever after seeing the world and understanding what I could hope to achieve. I worked hard, rarely took any leave, successfully passed various examinations for and was awarded various international licences, firmly established on my path to success.

No dream comes true until you wake up and go to work.
Anonymous

It was not all hard work though; some play was involved – it taught me to relax sometimes, and to take a load off my shoulders, to enjoy life while living it as well as working hard to achieve my goals. One cannot be in the merchant marine and not have some fun, as all seafarers do. Now that I look back, I can laugh heartily at the young man I was, so full of my own importance and so proud of my small achievements!

When I embarked upon my first voyage in 1964 at the age of twenty-one and proudly bearing the rank of Fifth Engineer, I was assigned to the MV *State of Andhra* (built in 1948), which was running between India and Japan via Singapore and Hong Kong, and a ship crewed by people who had no connections higher up to give them a more pleasant ship. Our Captain was a Welshman named Trevor, who 'stopped ageing' when he reached the retirement age of sixty and, to prove his point, visited the shipping office dressed as a Boy Scout. The Chief Engineer, Joseph, and he were both elderly men, and held true to the traditions of seamanship and its superstitions, including (so the rumours said) keeping a wife or a girlfriend in each port. On boarding the ship as a green young officer, I was promptly confronted by the Captain, in tune with the practice of ensuring that young recruits, and especially young officers, were instantly aware of the traditions. I was questioned about the state of my education in the 'feminine experience' department. They used several fairly explicit terms that I did not at the time understand and, when they realised that I had not yet lost my 'innocence', there was a great deal of muttering about 'bad luck sails with the ship'.

The upshot of all this questioning and rumblings among 'more experienced' seamen was that, when we reached Kobe, Japan instead of staying with the others on board, to mind matters while the senior officers took shore leave, I was told to accompany the radio officer into Kobe. After being shown a few of the sights and told not to worry about expenses (I had no money with me), I was eventually led like a lamb to slaughter into a bar in Kobe. One of the few hundred nightclubs and bars originally set up to entertain Japanese soldiers during World War II, this particular establishment was run by a Korean *mama-san*. The radio officer sat me down at a table, got me a beer, and walked off to talk to the lady overseeing the bar. After some intense conversation, apparently bargaining about the price, because he had brought a 'cherry boy' with him, he came back with a young and pretty Japanese girl. It was only in places like this where girls spoke broken English; otherwise in those days, it was difficult to communicate with the Japanese. I was introduced to the girl and told she would 'take care of me' that night. He then left me, the proverbial sacrificial lamb, to be 'educated' as befitted a seaman. I had to sacrifice my 'cherry boy' status in order to save the ship from the possibility of bad luck.

A few months later in 1965, when I went strolling around the town to admire the flowering trees in *Sakura* (cherry blossom) season with my senior colleague, Parampal Sidhu, we came across a group of pretty girls, full of blithe laughter. In comparison to him, I must have seemed a green young lad, for they pointed at me and chanted 'Cherry boy!' over and over again – it was only some time later that we realised what they really meant, but sadly we could not go back to show them how wrong they were.

A few months into my career, while I was still serving on the same ship, our Second Engineer, Mr Upadhyay (a short man, around five feet four) met and married a lovely Japanese lady (tall and willowy at five feet ten), and the entire ship's crew acted as the groom's entourage. At his wedding, it was my lucky day. I met a girl who was the daughter of a retired Colonel from the Japanese Army, who had served during the Second World War in the Andaman Islands. I met her again when the crew hosted a party aboard the ship, and pretty soon we embarked upon a full-blown relationship. She would meet me at the first Japanese port at which we docked in Japan, and then follow the ship, meeting me at every subsequent one. She would wash and sew for me and, since I spent long hours in the engine room as a junior on the ship, I used to ask my friend Parampal Sidhu, deck officer on the ship, to check on her from time to time to see if she needed anything. To this day he has been kept guessing whether it was because I trusted him or considered him harmless! This comfortable 'romance' carried on and, at the time of what was to be my last voyage to Japan aboard the MV *State of Andhra*, she expressed a desire for us to marry. I was a bit dubious, and also mindful that my family might object, so I told her that I would have to go back to India and speak with my mother. This I could honestly do, since I was planning to disembark in India in order to study for my Second Engineer's licence in late 1965.

Having signed off the crew register, I decided that going to Kanpur and being surrounded by my friends would be detrimental to my studious mood. I took my sabbatical and landed up at my eldest brother's house in Agra. He was, at the time, Director of the Tuberculosis Institute there, and the deciding factor was that he agreed to give me access to the extremely well-stocked Institute library. My sister-in-law's niece, Miss Manju Tandon (daughter of Mr DN Tandon, a leading criminal lawyer in the city of Bareilly, and Asha Lata, a famous singer of *bhajans* and religious songs), was staying with them at the time, studying for her BA in Agra. She was young, pretty and very interesting to talk to and although, in all honesty, neither of us can say that we fell instantly in love, there was enough of an attraction on my part to make me forget all about the Japanese girl I had left hanging around in Kobe – I imagine she soon tired of waiting for me and moved on to fairer pastures. I hope so. I was, perhaps, a little callous, but in my young heart there was definitely doubt about how well she would have fitted into my family and whether my family would have been comfortable with her as my wife. I should have written to her at least, I know, but I was young, and that was among my share of mistakes.

Manju and I, in the meantime, were getting to know each other very well indeed, and pretty quickly were deeply in love. I soon realised that this was the woman I wanted to spend the rest of my life with. I departed after being awarded my Second Engineer's Licence, aboard the MV *Amer Himalaya* on an India-Australia run, and we kept up a correspondence. Whenever the ship docked in port, I would dash across to my brother's house in Agra, where Manju and I would spend time together. On one of these visits, we decided we definitely wanted to marry each other, and both sets of parents gave their permission, surprising us by complacently telling us that they had quietly arranged for Manju to study in Agra in order to be able to meet me when I was visiting, in the hope that this very event might occur!

I wanted Manju to wait until January 1969, allowing time for me to study and then take the examination for my Chief Engineer's Licence, so that it would not cause any interference with our honeymoon. We decided that she should spend the two years until then studying for a BEd, which was a two-year course, mostly because I wanted her to be in Agra, so that I could meet her without any impediments. Our parents consulted a priest and set the date for the wedding in January 1969. It was then imperative for me to pass my examination at the first go.

I duly obtained the coveted Chief Engineer's Licence in December 1968 and I was the first (and probably still hold that record) to obtain this rank within four years of graduating from DMET. Manju and I were married on 29 January 1969, and my beloved wife has been a solid supporter of all activities and ventures in my life ever since – indeed, without her support and knack of stretching our income to meet our needs, I would have been hard-pressed indeed to succeed.

> *No man succeeds without a good woman behind him. Wife or mother, if it is both, he is twice blessed indeed.*
> Harold Macmillan

As the Indian merchant shipping industry expanded, the Shipping Corporation of India promoted me to the rank of Chief Engineer in September 1969. Since I was newly married at the time, a compassionate junior manager in the crewing department was, on his own initiative, trying to avoid assigning me to the post of Chief Engineer on the bulk carrier MV *Nalanda* (built in 1968), which was an unpopular posting, since the new bulk carriers did not stay long in port because they were speedily unloaded mechanically without docking. I was called to the office of the Director of the Crewing Department and asked point blank whether I had refused to take the posting. I was forthright and, since I had not asked the overzealous manager to assign me elsewhere, I confidently denied that I had refused to be assigned to the *Nalanda* and that I had not refused a single assignment in the five years that I had been with SCI.

I agreed to go, on one condition – that my wife was allowed to accompany me, in spite of the fact that wives at that time were only allowed on the ships when their husbands had completed at least one year of service after obtaining the relevant Licence, which I had not. The Director agreed, on his condition – that her papers were in order and did not delay my reporting date. Manju was with me in Mumbai at the time, having come from Kanpur for a few days to bid me farewell, and had with her only a handful of sarees and no documents whatsoever. She did not even own a passport. Armed with a recommendation from the Director of Administration of SCI, we headed to the passport office, and presented the completed forms along with the recommendation to the officer in charge. He grumbled that the Director had sent urgent cases like this once too often and telephoned him to complain – I must admit

I encouraged him to call, because I knew the Director would be away at lunch. To cut a long story short, he told us to collect the passport the next day, and our problems were solved. Poor Manju survived our entire tenure on the bulk carrier MV *Nalanda* for just under two years, and on a wardrobe of just eight sarees, when most Indian women cannot do without three times that number!

We disembarked in 1971, after a stint of twenty-two months without a single break at any port, because I was thinking of changing shipping companies – in order to complete my qualifications, I needed a term of experience on a steamship, having only served on a motor vessel up to that point. I was afraid that my career would be stunted due to the twenty-year waiting list for service on a steam-powered ship, of which SCI had only two at the time. However, when the Director at SCI heard that I wanted to resign, as he wanted me to stay because he felt I was an asset to the SCI; he lured me back by boosting me to the top of the waiting list for steamships. So, after disembarking in Japan (where Manju was keen to meet the Japanese girl I had 'dated', but was unable to locate), we returned to India for a month's holiday. I then joined a steam ship, the MV *State of Bombay*, running between Kolkata, the Andaman Islands and Chennai; it was during this tenure that my patriotism came to the fore once again, and I was able to serve my country in a small capacity. The *State of Bombay* was used in the Andaman Islands as a hospital ship for Indian defence service personnel during the Bangladesh war in early December 1971.

When we resumed commercial service after the fifteen-day war, our ship docked in Chennai. A telegram had been sent care of our agents and addressed to the Captain, instructing him to release me from my duties and send me to report to the Mumbai Head Office as Deputy Technical Manager on 22 December 1971 – thus I became the youngest manager at that time in the Shipping Corporation of India. It was a promotion gained by coming to the attention of my superiors, through two technical papers submitted during my sea service, which were being used as a basis for SCI's Planned Maintenance System for their fleet. Adding to my credit was my twenty-two month trouble-free run of the bulk carrier

MV *Nalanda*. I embarked on a new phase in life, as a management team-member, and my first dream came to life. At the relatively young age of thirty, this achievement led me to dream of an even greater future and to aim even higher than before.

> *There's nothing that can help you understand your beliefs more*
> *than trying to explain them to an inquisitive child.*
> Frank A. Clark

My personal life continued to be idyllic, and we were blessed with a son, who we named Saurabh, in 1971. That son now holds an MSc in Shipping & Trade Finance from Cass Business School, London is married to Neha and is himself blessed with a son and a daughter. My daughter Manjari was born in 1973 and today holds a BSc in Textile Marketing & Management from the University of Manchester, is married to Utsav, and blessed with three sons. In Bombay, we started family life in a company flat, which was a little restricted so, at weekends, as the children grew taller, and our rooms smaller, we took them to Juhu Beach, or Madh Island in Bombay.

My working life had begun well – with the right choices, a good plan, and a balance made possible by my marriage and new family. At a relatively early age, I had discovered how to make the best use of my time.

Above left: With the Third Engineer on my first voyage aboard the *MV State of Andhra*

Right: In my early days, probably taken when I was in Japan, judging by the car's numberplate

Below: Manju and I were engaged in 1965, but I asked her to wait a few years before getting married, since I wanted to finish my Chief Engineer's licence exam

Above left: I arrived at the wedding venue on 29th January 1969 in full traditional Indian regalia

Right: Manju and I get married

Below: My beautiful bride, Miss Manju Tandon

Above: I became Chief Engineer on the *MV Nalanda* in 1969

Right: In Chief Engineer's uniform in 1969

Below: Manju and our children, Manjari and Saurabh

Life Lesson Five

When opportunity knocks,
open the door.

OPEN YOUR EYES

Luck is what happens when preparation meets opportunity.

Seneca

I am convinced that the first step to recognising opportunities is to be open-minded. Anything is possible. When presented with an opportunity, hold your scepticism in check and explore the possibilities with an open mind. Opportunities cost time and money, and come in various forms: a sudden call from colleagues or friends, a tip from the newspapers, or any other medium. Always ask yourself 'How can I benefit from it?' When your subconscious mind truly believes that everything happens because of you and to your benefit, you will realise that, no matter how bad the situation, you can always benefit from it. Evaluate each opportunity, ask yourself whether the opportunity is consistent with your goal, and whether it can lead you to where you want to be? Are you excited and positive about the opportunity? You never knows where opportunity lies, when it's going to show up, what is going to be expected of you in order to take advantage of that opportunity, or what the outcome is going to be if you do take advantage of it. You also don't know if it's going to be worth your time or worth the risk involved. Yet, finding opportunity in your life and around you is vital to your success. Really good opportunities come and go in a heartbeat. Somebody else takes it or else it just passes by, and then you're still in the same spot you were in before. The truth of the matter is that opportunity is everywhere. Just open your eyes and LOOK.

When I joined the Head Office of the Shipping Corporation of India on 22 December 1971, I was restless, because having a desk job was a novelty. I told myself that I had to make the job interesting for myself and, feeling that many things seemed to be wrong, I wanted to correct everything and make it efficient. Within a few months I was identified as a troublemaker in the Company – I stirred things up, but I was also recognised as efficient and professional. The only interesting events were the activities conducted by the UK-based International Marine Engineers Association, for whom I organised the Thirtieth Anniversary Conference in Mumbai. Having created a stir and thereby attracted the attention of my superiors, in December 1973 I was transferred to a post where I was out of their way, and was put in charge of supervising and operating all the ships owned by the Government of India and managed by SCI – the least profitable division, and one which no one else wanted to handle since the chances of promotion were negligible. There were about thirty ships in this category, mainly passenger vessels for various islands, lighthouse ships, plus a fleet of eight dredgers.

> *We are all faced with a series of great opportunities brilliantly disguised as impossible situations.*
> Charles R Swindoll

The Ministry of Shipping had initially bought the dredgers for capital dredging work at existing ports and to create new ones. As India was (and still is) short of port capacity for the loading and unloading of cargo ships, I looked upon this as an opportunity to shine. I asked myself what it would take to make the dredging fleet of the Government of India a productive one – I was in charge of these ships for three years and, during that period there were a number of opportunities, of each of which I took full advantage.

One of the major highlights was the berthing for the first time ever, of the world-famous cruise liner *Queen Elizabeth II* (*QEII*) at Ballard Pier in Mumbai. The Peninsular & Orient Shipping Line (Cunard ship) had charted her world cruise course, and had clearly stated that they wanted her to dock at the port and not in anchorage, making this their condition for bringing her to India. The Mumbai port was in a pitiable state in 1973 when the request came, and needed dredging within the extremely short time left before the liner arrived in 1975. There was a typical bureaucratic situation with endless meetings where discussions carried on and went nowhere, and the Mumbai Port Authority, which was supposed to do the dredging, was avoiding the issue. I was invited by the Chairman of the Mumbai Port Authority to one such meeting and, frustrated by the bureaucratic tangle, I volunteered to take on the project. This was apparently an unusual stance for an SCI representative to take, and the Ministry official jumped at the chance to actually make progress. He said that, if I was that interested in the challenge, I could take responsibility for it. I agreed, with the stipulation that I wanted complete autonomy and a sizeable budget to complete the project. The job was technical, complicated and had a deadline – just the sort of work I was hankering after, to soothe my restless brain!

Never work just for money or for power. They won't save your soul or help you sleep at night.
Marian Wright Edelman

This was the first project during which I experienced the warm feeling that power and money bestow. Despite the heady feeling it induced, I took the responsibility seriously, having already learned from my rustication in college that I could not take undue risks with my career. We finished well ahead of time, and brought an important client into the Shipping Corporation of India's fold – the Government of India, who officially owned the dredgers we operated, but still had to pay us all the costs. Among the many projects they granted to us after the success of the dredging at Mumbai Port were the deepening of the outer harbour of Port Vizag for iron ore export on seventy-five thousand ton ships (an upgrade from the thirty-five thousand ton ships that were then being used), and the creation of a new harbour at Mangalore. By the time I had completed these projects and made the dredging division profitable, we were showing a profit of around ten paisa (one-tenth of a rupee) per cubic foot of sand excavated – in 1973-74 alone, the Shipping Corporation of India earned a commission of thirty million (three crore) Indian rupees. With that, the Government of India suddenly woke up to the profitability of the whole enterprise, and decided to create the Dredging Corporation of India in late 1974. This had the immediate result that they took their dredgers away from the Shipping Corporation of India and, consequently, from me. Although the Ministry of Shipping was impressed with my performance so far, and was keen that, even at the young age of thirty-three, I should apply for the post of Chairman and Managing Director of the new company, the Shipping Corporation of India found the suggestion preposterous. Yet fortune smiled upon me again – another challenge was on its way.

Opportunity had come knocking – it seemed it had sought me out. My door was open, and I both saw it and grabbed it. One thing really does lead to another and the next opportunity was not far away, so what started as an instinct became a habit.

RMS Queen Elizabeth 2

Above: The QE2 which docked at Mumbai

Below: One of the events I organised when I was 'being disruptive' at the Head Office of the Shipping Corporation of India in Mumbai was the 30th Anniversary Conference of the International Marine Engineers' Association

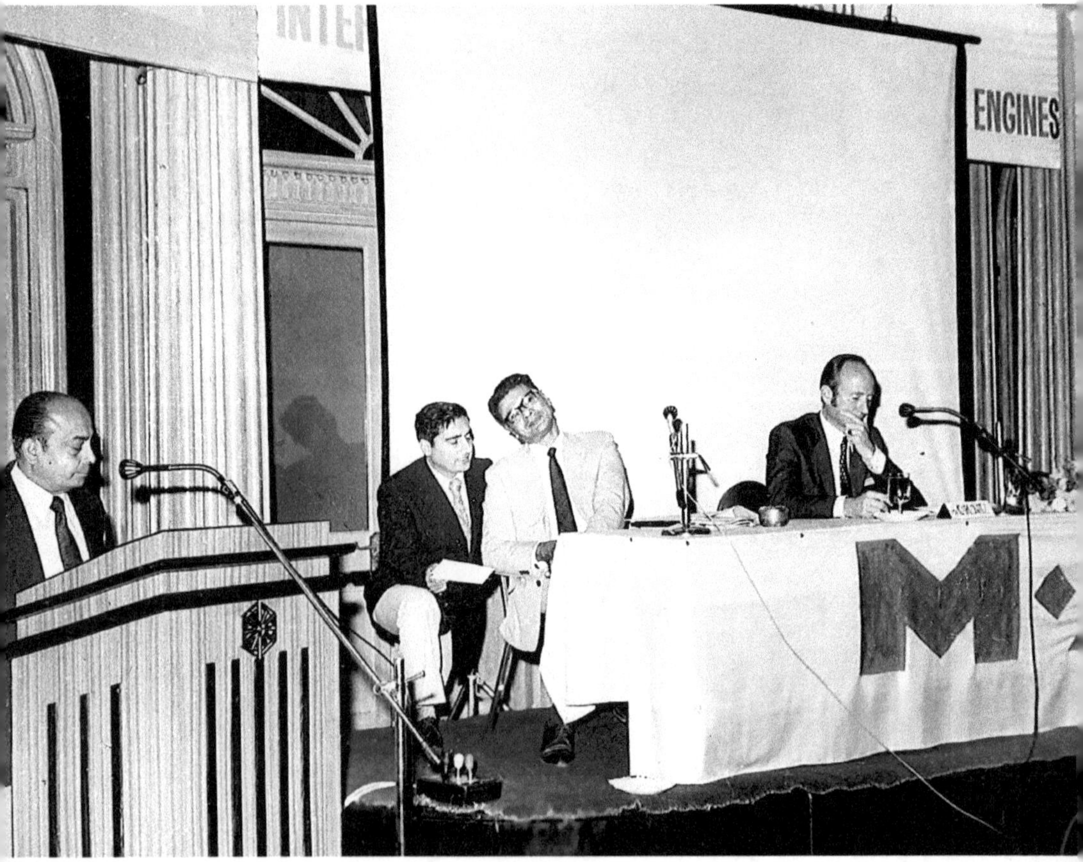

Life Lesson Six

Every challenge is an opportunity,
so risk it and win it.

RISK IS RIGHT

*Do not fear risk. All exploration, all growth is calculated. Without [a]
challenge people cannot reach their higher selves. Only if we are willing to
walk over the edge can we become winners.*

Anonymous

I have often read that, according to experts, 'the ability to take calculated risks is an essential human trait, crucial to our development as a species and as individuals'. Our risk-taking ancestors were the survivors, the daring ones who took chances in order to adapt to a changing environment and today the same principle applies. To grow, we need to experience challenges; it's an experience crucial for anyone who wants to be emotionally resilient, confident, happy, and engaged with life. You just have to give more attention to those areas that feel challenging – and intriguing – to you, and embrace the adventure of uncertainty. 'Do one thing every day that scares you', Eleanor Roosevelt once said. On the other side of that fear, opportunity awaits. Risks form the adventurous aspect of our otherwise dull and boring existence. The idea of taking risks does not appeal to everyone, but those who truly believe in reaching for the sky often realise early in their lives that it would be impossible for them to do so if they did not take any risks. The maximum that can happen is failure but, if you are bold enough to take risks, do not get intimidated by the mere fear of failure. Having encountered failure once, your chances of success will be higher at the next attempt because, not only will you be cautious about the mistakes that you committed the first time round, you will also be in a position to make a better choice regarding the methods and strategies to be used. It is extremely important to ensure that you take only calculated risks, which enable you to inch closer towards your goal, rather than wild conjectures which would leave you worse off than you were before.

In 1974, the then Prime Minister of India, Mrs Indira Gandhi, and Iran's king at that time, Reza Shah Pahlavi, signed a protocol for the development of the Kudremukh Iron Ore Mines and the export of this iron ore to Iran. The Shah insisted that there must be a joint venture shipping company to transport the iron ore to Iran. He also requested that the headquarters of the shipping company be in Iran since the mining headquarters were in India. The Government of India and the SCI Panel selected me as second-in-command of the team that went to Iran in April 1975, as founder members of the Irano Hind Shipping Company, a joint venture shipping company, fifty-one percent owned by Iran and the remainder by India; its day-to-day operations were to be managed by two national shipping lines – Arya National Lines of Iran and the Shipping Corporation of India. When our team, comprising Managing Director Mr P.C. Shukla and four Managers, arrived in Iran, we brought with us a cheque from the Government of India, comprising their share of the million dollar equity – four hundred and ninety thousand US dollars. For the first two years, the management of this joint venture was to be undertaken by SCI and our team's job was to establish the shipping company and operate it profitably. According to the constitution of the joint venture, the posts of Chairman and Managing Director would be shared by Iran and India in alternating two-year terms.

> *Often the difference between a successful person and a failure is not one has better abilities or ideas, but the courage that one has to bet on one's ideas, to take a calculated risk – and to act.*
> Andre Malraux

We arrived in Iran and sublet offices from the Arya National Shipping Line of Iran; we had to stock up on everything from furniture to utensils and stationery, and establish the Company. At the same time, I wanted a family home with space for the children, but company policy meant allowable rents were too tight for a villa or a ground floor apartment. Then some friends helped me find a newly built villa in Zargandeh, a village only accessible by mud road. Nonetheless, it had a large garden and the rent was reasonable, so that is where we settled down and where, to get a taxi to work, I had to trudge through the village and up to the main road. Today that village has disappeared as part of a greater Teheran.

Having completed the set-up, we were then told that the Kudremukh Iron Ore Mines project had been delayed by two years. This created a dilemma, because our million dollar capital would certainly not survive that long. Managing Director Mr P.C. Shukla was the most senior executive director at SCI, and his ambition was to become its Chairman after his two year posting with Irano Hind. It was therefore important to him that the Company took off and added a shine to his *curriculum vitae*. We were told that our immediate goal was to make Irano Hind profitably operational, using our own ships, and before the end of his tenure in two years' time. The question now was funding – in the 1970s, a second-hand ship cost a minimum of ten million US dollars whereas today they cost over sixty million. The task of establishing a shipping company with its own ships was almost impossible, given our capital was only one million US dollars.

The team was unable to come up with any ideas, and it was here that I saw an opportunity to bring myself to the notice of my superiors once again as a man with solutions to every problem -and possibly to be appointed the next Managing Director of Irano Hind after Mr Shukla. If I could prove myself, the eternal bureaucratic system of seniority at SCI might no longer be an issue.

Obtaining soft funding from the government of the Shah of Iran was vital, so I prepared a project report for the Iranian Ministry of Finance to assist the Irano Hind Shipping Company, by providing a 100 million US dollar loan. Under the rule of the Shah, each ministry had an American Advisor, who was the first port of call before any minister could be approached. Accordingly, Irano Hind's Finance Manager and I met with the Advisor to the Finance Minister of Iran, who told me very clearly that he thought it was a mistake to have formed a joint venture shipping company with India. His opinion, frankly and clearly stated was 'If you form a joint venture it should be between parties in which one has the know-how and the other has the finance. Iran has the finance but India does not have the knowledge of high calibre shipping'. In conclusion, he said that he had written to the Shah through his Minister, stating that this joint venture should be terminated, as it was unlikely to prosper. 'Therefore,' he said, humiliatingly, 'there is no need for you to meet the Finance Minister.'

Don't wait for extraordinary opportunities. Seize common occasions and make them great. Weak men wait for opportunities; strong men make them.
Orison Swett Marden

That episode simply fired me up, so I decided that I needed other resources to get the Company up and running. I knew that I had to succeed in establishing its profitability at all costs. I suggested to the Managing Director that we should approach parent company SCI and ask it to charter one of its ships to us for six months. That would enable us to avoid paying the charter hire guarantee, which other companies would demand and which we could not afford. No-one in the team wanted to take the proposal to SCI, so I volunteered, again putting myself in the firing line – and the limelight. For a technical manager such as I to propose such a scheme to the department manager and the executive department director of SCI was quite a task. I flew to Mumbai, remained there for three weeks, and returned to Tehran, having succeeded in chartering a ship for six months. Once the basic agreement had been signed, it was handed over to the Commercial Manager of Irano Hind to work out the details. My two-fold aim had been achieved – we had got a ship, and I had been noticed by my superiors.

The pessimist sees difficulty in every opportunity. The optimist sees the opportunity in every difficulty.
Winston Churchill

An unusual by-product of the charter agreement greatly improved my plotting, planning, anticipatory and strategic skills. Since we did not want this ship to sail without a cargo from India to Iran, we loaded up at Kolkata port with a cargo of tea from India and Sri Lanka and jute from Bangladesh. By the time the ship reached Iranian waters and was ready to dock at the busy port of Khorramshahr, there was a long waiting list of ships and it could have taken more than six months to dock, and offload the cargo; we were looking at heavy losses rather than the expected profit. The Iranian Chairman of our Company did all he could to help, but hinted that more could be done if we could find someone with 'blue-blood' from the Shah's extensive family to intervene.

We found Prince Shaffiq, a nephew of the Shah, and a Commander in the Iranian Royal Navy, who also loved Darjeeling tea, and asked him if he would inaugurate the first Darjeeling cargo to arrive in Iran. We then co-ordinated the dates and pressured the Port Director into giving us a one day window to dock, so that the inauguration could be completed. He agreed grudgingly, but insisted that the ship must go back to its place immediately after the ceremony. During the inauguration, I mentioned casually to the Prince that all the wonderful tea in our cargo hold would lose its flavour because we were so far down the docking queue. Right on cue, he was horrified and told us to offload all the tea, within hearing of the Port Director; when we mentioned the time constraints, he spoke to the Port Director in Persian and ordered him to let us stay.

We were given seventy-two hours and it was then my aim to ensure that not only the tea but the rest of our cargo was safely offloaded. I did my share of manual labour in order to finish on time, hoping that we would succeed against all odds. In those days, without advanced technology, offloading ten thousand tonnes of cargo took nearly ten days. Fortunately for us, my hands-on approach impressed the port labourers and they were more enthusiastic about helping me to achieve my objective; we completed unloading in seventy hours, with two hours to spare. We gave hefty bonuses to all the port labourers, plus a packet of Darjeeling tea – they were all very pleased!

Labour was the first price, the original purchase – money that was paid for all things. It was not by gold or by silver, but by labour, that all wealth of the world was originally purchased.
Adam Smith

Now that Irano Hind was operating commercially and profitably, half the battle was won, but we still needed to buy ships and build up our fleet, bearing in mind the deadline set by our Managing Director's ambitions, and to complete our mission. To do so we turned to our principal partner, the Arya National Shipping Line of Iran. They had a subsidiary called South Shipping Lines, which was disposing of four of their old tween-deckers (general cargo-carrying ships), whose average age was eighteen years, which left only around two more years of seaworthiness. We decided to persuade ANSL to bare-boat charter them to Irano-Hind for a four year period on a hire-purchase basis. This meant hiring them out without crew or provisions for what was effectively rental income, just as modern yacht brokers rent out pleasure craft for others to skipper and the well-off to hire, rather than buy their own. SCI discouraged us from doing so since the ships were near the end of their useful life, telling us that we would not be able to manage them profitably due to lack of expertise and resources – we were after all only a four-man team at Irano Hind. However, we were determined to get the ships, since there was no other way to obtain younger vessels without a bank guarantee or our own funds. Mr Shukla's ambitions overruled SCI's decree and he told me that, if I was willing to go to see the ships and considered them technically suitable, he would force the deal on the Board.

You learn something every day if you pay attention.
Ray LeBlond

The four ships were anchored far outside the jurisdiction of Khorramshahr port. I could not find official transportation to take me to see them because they were outside the port's limits, so I hired a fisherman and his small boat. He took me upriver from Shut-al-Arab and then to sea, but the journey took some time, added to which I had to fix his engine, which failed *en route*. I also had to survive on palm dates for more than a day and a half, which was a learning experience in itself – I now know there are several varieties of dates in existence, and the ones from Basra were my favourites. That was a short but memorable journey, but I will always remember it because it taught me that you can learn everywhere and in any situation and gain odd nuggets of information in the most unexpected places.

We bought those ships, based on my report, on hire-purchase. They remained profitably operational until 1987 – over ten years! Other problems arose, but none so great that they were insurmountable. Instead, in learning to make the Irano Hind Shipping Company profitable, I was accumulating a wealth of knowledge that I would draw upon years lat*er* when setting up my own company, Foresight Limited. I worked hard – day and night – travelling to see ships, buying, hiring and generally doing my best to make the venture a success, by using both my knowledge of shipping and my connections. Eventually, from September 1976 to March 1980, I held five concurrent positions at Irano Hind – as Manager Fleet Management & Personnel, Manager Technical, Manager Project Development, Manager Planning, and Manager Public Relations.

While we were in Iran, Manju, the children and I decided to take advantage of the ten-day holiday around the Iranian New Year in March 1978, and took a road trip to Afghanistan, thinking of it as a good opportunity for a sailor and his family to visit a landlocked country. Having loved fruit since my childhood, I was also looking forward to seeing the lands of Chaman and Kandahar, where the sweetest grapes and pomegranates grew.

We went by car, and temperatures were high during the day, and as low as 6 degrees centigrade at night. It was high noon, one day, and

Manju was driving us towards Kandahar. I was sitting in the passenger seat with Manjari in my lap, and Saurabh and our maid were seated in the back seat. The Asian Highway, connecting Turkey to the Khyber pass, was narrow, and not a dual carriageway. The heat got to Manju, who was driving quite fast; she saw a mirage and felt suddenly dizzy, and swerved off the road, overturning the car into the ditch. I crawled out, looking for Manjari, who had hit her head on the dashboard and been thrown out through the windshield. Saurabh and our maid were severely bruised, but Manju was lying over the steering wheel, unconscious. Terror stuck my heart – what if I had lost her?

We were in a strange land, with no-one nearby, and no medical help at all. Even in that state of shock, my subconscious act was to pick up Manju's handbag, which contained our passports and cash, and had gone flying when the car crashed. I began to wave at passing trucks and cars, in an attempt to make them stop and help – it was only then that I realised my right shoulder was immobile. At length, a truck stopped, and the labourers helped us to lay Manju down on its cargo of pebbles. We climbed into the truck as well, and they took us to a hospital in Khandhar, where the Manju and Manjari were revived and given rudimentary first aid, without even local anaesthesia. To this day, our frozen shoulders – Manju's left and my right – and a fine s-shaped scar on Manjari's forehead (where her cut was sewn with thirty-six stitches) stand as a constant reminder of the narrow escape from death of my most precious cargo – my family.

The events I have narrated marked the beginning of over three decades of success for the Irano-Hind Shipping Company. Working initially with multi-purpose vessels, Irano Hind soon moved into reefer (refrigerated) ship chartering and buying, taking over much of the Iranian market from the then dominant European companies – Blue Star and Salen Reefers – through whom Iran imported beef from Australia and New Zealand (the Iranians are very fond of kebabs). My memories of those days are as bright as ever. I worked so hard to make Irano Hind a success, and all that effort paid off. Even today, the Company is still a profitable international shipping company and India has enjoyed dividends every year since its inception in 1975, the only low point being 1979, the year of the Iranian Revolution.

It was a time of challenge – and risks. Ambition, coupled perhaps with the innocence of youth, compelled me to take risks, calculating more would be lost if I did not, and those risks paid off, as risks taken with care and calculation invariably do.

Above: At my desk at the Irano Hind offices in Tehran, Iran, late 1970s

Below: Manju plays the harmonium at the DMET Annual Entertainment program in April 1975. Ex-cadet Mukhopadhyay got it together on the tabla

Above: I strike a pose at the port of Khorramshahr in Iran, shortly after the Iran-Iraq war

Right: A casual photograph, taken in Iran when I still smoked a pipe

Below: Darjeeling tea

ORGANIC TEA

Life Lesson Seven

Face conflict, confront it, for it's not
something to be afraid of.

FACE THE FIGHT

*The harder the conflict, the more glorious the triumph. What we obtain
too cheap, we esteem too lightly; it is dearness only that gives everything its
value. I love the man that can smile in trouble, that can gather strength
from distress and grow.*

Thomas Paine

One of the more common definitions of conflict is that it is a clash between opposing groups or that it is a power struggle or a battle between opposing forces. Some of you may go so far as to believe that, were it not for other people, you would never have to deal with conflict. I feel that it is easy to blame a conflict on an external force (another person, an event beyond your control), but the reason you are experiencing conflict is because you are not reconciled to your role. It really is important for you to know the true nature of any conflict you are facing. In my experience, as you become more aware of what causes you to feel conflicted, you will become more aware of the best way to handle yourself when you experience conflict. You cannot control the actions of others; you can only control your own actions. All leaders have to deal with conflict. If you don't want to deal with conflict, leadership is not your thing. Being a leader is not about IF you will tackle conflict but HOW; as Confucius said, 'A leader must be a dealer in hope'. In fact, no other ability (other than being able to get results) so shapes one's career as the ability to deal with conflict. Conflict and leadership go hand-in-hand because leadership involves challenging people often to do what they don't want to do – you should not always take 'no' for an answer. Achieving goals involves people having to get out of their comfort zones, making troublesome decisions, and engaging in disconcerting new actions. Leadership helps guide and motivate people to do those things. My aim has always been to stay focused on results – it works.

It was either my propensity to gravitate towards troubled situations that brought me face-to-face with my destiny or the fact that my destiny was to create successes out of troubled situations. Nevertheless, whatever is the answer to that, I have always felt that there is a connection there, and I have created my destiny by facing 'troubled situations' head-on. It's not always that strife, war and revolutions can be beneficial. Yet another hotbed of trouble leading to a challenge, and thence success, popped up in my life in 1979, when Iranian leader Ayatollah Khomeini arrived in Iran to lead the Revolution. I remained in what became the Islamic Republic of Iran, running the Irano Hind Shipping Company and could not leave without handing responsibility for the joint venture to someone officially designated by both the countries involved. So, although a few of my associates returned to India, my family and I remained in the Islamic Republic of Iran during the Revolution.

It was risky, and I was told it would be a good idea to leave Zargandeh for security reasons, and to move into the heart of the city. Luckily for us, during the Shah's reign, the Israelis had built a large, gated complex of 11 buildings, each 11 storeys high, with its own garden, swimming pool and gym. The Israelis had left, so I persuaded the authorities to allot me one of those flats. We got No 9 on the 11th floor, a huge three-bedroom apartment with maid's room, and a gated garden staffed by security guards. The children were safe, though they were not there that often, except during the school holidays.

> *An adventure is only an inconvenience rightly considered. An*
> *inconvenience is only an adventure wrongly considered.*
> G.K. Chesterton

One day, soon after the Revolution had begun, Islamic guards were sent to escort me to Revolutionary Council Headquarters. I was petrified. The Revolutionaries were allegedly executing people related to or connected with the Shah of Iran. I called Mr Ali Akbar Khalili, then the Indian Ambassador in Tehran and both he and the Managing Director of Irano Hind advised me to go. When I reached the Headquarters, they surprised me by producing a complete dossier on me. They further astonished me by telling me that since the Islamic Republic of Iran did not have an oil pipeline and all oil (more than three million barrels per day) was exported by sea from Kharg Island, shipping lanes for oil exports would have to be kept open to fund the Revolution. Ayatollah Khomeini was therefore demanding the appointment of a Principal Advisor on Shipping to the Chairman and Managing Director of the Arya National Shipping Lines, who was 'neither Iranian, nor Muslim, nor European, nor American'. The Revolutionary Council wanted me to fill the position and asked me to name my terms. I refused, saying that I was an employee of the Government of India, deputed to run the Irano Hind Shipping Company. My other concern was that, if I took the post, they would nationalise my baby, the Irano Hind Shipping Company, as they had been doing to all commercial, industrial and financial joint venture institutions in Iran. They asked me what I wanted and I made it clear that they would have to gain permission from the Government of India for my services, and also guarantee that they would not nationalise the Company. I was escorted back to my office and left on my own. Within a week the escort returned and took me once again to Headquarters. I was told that my terms were acceptable and an emissary had been sent to New Delhi to obtain the permission required. They could not guarantee that they would not nationalise the Irano-Hind Shipping Company but assured me that they would do everything in their power to prevent it.

Nothing in life is to be feared. It is only to be understood.
Marie Curie

I was returned to my office once more and, within seventy-two hours, received telephone calls from the Indian Ministry of Shipping and the then Chairman of the Shipping Corporation of India Admiral Kishan Dev, saying that the Prime Minister (at that time, Morarji Desai) was pleased to have an Indian as Principal Advisor on Shipping in Iran. They said India was honoured by the request, and my services were to be loaned to the Government of the Islamic Republic.

So, there I was, in October 1979, having been appointed Principal Advisor on Shipping to the Government of the Islamic Republic of Iran. I, who had been rusticated and expelled from DMET in 1961 for excessive ragging, had become the most senior foreigner in post-revolutionary Iran. Even Ambassadors of other countries had to seek an appointment with me if they had any issues related to shipping! My first task was to nationalise the Arya National Shipping Line which I, and indeed most others, had been under the mistaken impression was already nationalised. This was not the case – it was owned by the Shah's foundation. I took responsibility for nationalising the line and it became the Islamic Republic of Iran Shipping Lines (IRISL) – I personally drew up the bill of nationalisation, in order to ensure that it would remain the country's premier shipping organisation. I also became Principal Advisor, and Mr Abdul Ali Erfani, who was then the Deputy Minister of Commerce, was appointed Chairman and Managing Director.

Shortly after I took up the position of Principal Advisor, both Pakistan and Bangladesh sent several high-powered delegations to Iran to persuade the Government to create more joint venture companies along the same lines as the Irano Hind Shipping Company. At great personal risk, I succeeded in deterring the Government of the Islamic Republic from accepting these proposals, based on my loyalty to my own country and to Irano Hind Shipping, both of which would have suffered had the agreements been made. Had these companies been formed, they would also have been highly detrimental to the future of the Irano Hind Shipping Company, which I had worked so hard to build up. The Bangladesh venture, especially, would have demolished the fortunes of Irano Hind. A major source of our income was tea (voluminous but light cargo) imported from Kolkata, and the ships would no longer have had the base cargo of raw jute (providing ballast to the voluminous but light cargo of tea), which ensured the profitability of the venture, if Bangladesh began exporting it as well.

*Don't waste life in doubts and fears; spend yourself on the work
before you, well assured that the right performance of this hour's
duties will be the best preparation for the hours and ages that will
follow it.*
Ralph Waldo Emerson

I also found, having met him a few times during the course of my tenure, that Ayatollah Khomeini was an intelligent and capable person, who recognised the importance of shipping to ensure the continuous inflow of petro-dollars. I was given a free hand in re-organising IRISL and funds were freely available for development too, because a high-powered Finance Committee had been deputed for the purpose. The Company had been running at a severe loss and I needed all the tact, knowledge and experience at my disposal to make this concern a 'money-spinner'. I applied my imagination and expertise, and reorganised the workings of the Company to meet international standards, reallocated the fleet to more promising sectors to ensure better returns, computerised their records to keep tabs on results, and in general tried to improve their overall performance.

During the Iran-Iraq War that began in September 1980, many Indian sailors and their families were trapped along the Shut-al-Arab River with no means of getting home to India. My proudest achievement was ensuring that they were all flown back to India. I also persuaded post-revolutionary Iran to buy Indian jeeps, since American ones had been banned by the Revolutionary Council as part of the cessation of all dealings with the USA. It was the Iranians, however, who persuaded Indian manufacturers to put in better engines and therefore make the jeeps more popular. As a patriot and individual Indian, I welcomed the chance to help my country, Mother India.

During those first four years up to 1984 Manju shuttled between Teheran and India, where the children were at school, every two months. Saurabh at nine years old and six year old Manjari went to Manju's family home at Bareilly. For their first year they joined an English Medium school, St Maria Goretti High School, and later, residential schools in

Nainital, a hill station around 90km from Bareilly. Saurabh went to St Joseph's and Manjari attended All Saints College.

It was a critical time for IRISL, four ships had been devastated in the first days of the Iran-Iraq war in late September 1980, and the ports of Bushehr and Khorramshahr, among others, were under repeated attack. In 1981, Mr M. Souri (who had also been Deputy Minister of Commerce) took over as Chairman and Managing Director of IRISL from Mr Erfani, who was unwell. During his tenure, we purchased or ordered seventy-two ships, some new or commissioned and some second-hand. Mr Souri remains a good friend to this day.

Mr Nezam Zeineddin, Director of Fleet and Administration, also soon became a good friend, and we used to exchange our lunches every day – he would eat my Indian food and I would eat his delicious Iranian delicacies.

As a result of my efforts and the free hand I was granted, I wore dual caps in a career that had suddenly taken on a new dimension. I also facilitated the creation of an entirely new port at Chabahar (on the Iran-Pakistan border), which provided employment to the formerly neglected locals in the Baluchistan area. This made them more co-operative and the Iranian Government was pleased. I took the opportunity to convince them that setting up a Maritime Institute there would also be an excellent idea – as a result, the fishermen of the region were trained as sailors and, as of 2009, all three hundred ships going to foreign shores and owned by Iran were manned by a full Iranian crew.

> I claim not to have controlled events, but confess plainly that
> events have controlled me.
> Abraham Lincoln

I travelled all over Iran, especially the coastal areas, even during the war years to Chabahar, Bandar Abbas, Bushehr, Bandar Imam Khomeini and Hendejan among other places, building up Iran's shipping fleet. I even remember that, with Mr Nezam Zeinedden translating into Persian, we wrote a collection of articles around that time on the basics and technical aspects of shipping, which became fairly popular in Iran when serialised in the national monthly shipping magazine. Unfortunately, though we wanted to publish them as a book, we were unable to do so. I also take pride in my contribution to Iran's expansion of the Chabahar docks, setting up a marine college and training of seafarers.

When I took over as Principal Advisor on Shipping in 1979, Iran had twenty-eight ships and, when I left five years later in August 1984, I had developed the fleet to one hundred and thirty- one ships. With that nucleus, the Iranian Shipping Fleet today is bigger than India's own merchant fleet. In August 1982, the Governments of India and the Islamic Republic of Iran recognised my contribution to shipping in Iran, and unanimously nominated me to the post of Managing Director of Irano Hind for a two year period, succeeding Mr L.M.S. Rajawar. My good friend and colleague Nezam Zeineddin was assigned to me as an advisor, and we worked efficiently together on a number of projects. We also travelled extensively and he helped me, during my tenure, to expand the fleet and diversify its operations, including operating reefer vessels for the first time in the history of the country. He was involved in public relations and cargo sectors while I focused on technical details and chartering.

In 1984, *Lloyd's List* and the International Chamber of Commerce asked me to speak at an important conference on Maritime Joint Ventures, the aim of which was to bring together experts, to hammer out practical ways of implementing the UN-sponsored Caracas Declaration on joint ventures, cutting across national boundaries. This was my first opportunity to speak at an international level. It was a new experience and one that I was quite apprehensive about – I was uncertain whether or not to accept because, even though I was running a joint venture myself, I did not think I could speak on 'The Risk Element in Joint Ventures'. When I shared my doubts with my wife Manju, she laughed and said 'Isn't our marriage the first joint venture of our lives?' And that set me thinking. It's true that the first joint venture in life is the marriage between a man and a woman and their determination to make it a success, which has greater risk in developing countries since the two parties are not always acquainted with each other. Manju also pointed out to me that the very basis of the survival of the human race is the ability of people to rely on people – beginning with one's parents, then one's spouse or partner, and finally on one's children. I realised that I could point out that the secret to the success of a joint venture lies in sincerity and a willingness to sacrifice and share. The very next day, I sent a message to Roy Baker, the Conference Director, and confirmed that I would speak at the conference.

That same year, as my tenure was coming to an end, the Shipping Corporation of India wanted to recall me to India, because of increasing concern over my alleged power in Iran. Though the two year term of office of the Managing Director of Irano Hind was supposed to rotate between an Indian and Iranian, we Indians had been left to carry on, as we were doing so well. The Government of the Islamic Republic wanted me to continue but SCI was so exasperated by the loyalty shown me, they preferred to have an Iranian take his turn, so I was told to return to India.

Keep away from those who try to belittle your ambitions. Small people always do that, but the really great make you believe that you too can become great.
Mark Twain

My ambition has always moved me to make something of myself, and that is a good thing. It is good to strive to be the best you can, to achieve prominence and understanding, and on an activity that is worthy of spending your life honourably. Ambition means more than a mere eagerness for things – it means the deep-seated desire to materialise one's dreams, an eager desire, not a mere wish for it, but a fierce, eager, consuming hunger which demands satisfaction – it is a good thing and not something of which to be ashamed. I always urge it on, feed it, and stimulate its growth. I never let the argument that men have used ambition to accomplish evil ends disconcert me. Every natural law is capable of being used for good or evil.

Company politics led me to leave Iran but, to be honest, when I first thought of leaving it was not with the intention of creating my own shipping company. When the Iranian Revolution took place, all English-medium schools were closed and I had to move my children to a boarding school in India. My wife was shuttling between the two countries, and it was playing havoc with our personal lives. When I considered my options with a clear head, I realised that, after having the kind of power and status that I had enjoyed in Iran for all those years, I could not go back to the Shipping Corporation of India in a senior managerial position – I would have to take a massive step down the career ladder. Although my expertise was not in question my age was, and that would stand in my way.

I instantly realised that this was an opportunity for me to change from being a professional to being an entrepreneur and I did not want to miss the opportunity. It was a revelation; the fire began to burn in my belly again and I knew that all I had really ever wanted was to have my own company and my own ships, answerable to no-one but my clients. In addition, while Ayatollah Khomeini's office realised that it was not in my nature to accept any bonus or compensation, they said that any time I needed business assistance they would provide it – something I realised later could be of considerable use in my entrepreneurial career.

You've got to go out on a limb sometimes because that's where the fruit is.
Will Rogers

In 1979 I had needed the Government of India's support to accept the post of Principal Advisor on Shipping to the Government of the Islamic Republic of Iran. Now, in 1984, I needed the Government of the Islamic Republic of Iran's help to be released quickly from the Shipping Corporation of India in order to pursue my entrepreneurial urge. In those days, the bureaucracy stipulated that an officer could not resign from posts outside India – I had to return to my home country and resign from my original local post. The bureaucratic labyrinths made this difficult, but I managed to convince the officials concerned that I would step down as Managing Director of Irano Hind if they would accept my resignation from the Shipping Corporation of India with immediate effect. It was agreed that I would be released within twenty-four hours once I arrived in India and I submitted my resignation to the Chairman of the Shipping Corporation of India.

One doesn't discover new lands without consenting to lose sight of the shore for a very long time.
Andre Gide

I handed over in Iran on 22 August 1984 and arrived in Mumbai the next day. I resigned on 23 August, my resignation was accepted with immediate effect, and I flew out of Mumbai on 24 August to London as a budding entrepreneur – full of ideas but with empty pockets.

Iran was a time of conflicts – the Revolution, international competition, war, and company politics. It was also a time to fight, with determination born of ambition. The fight was fought – and won.

Above: A few associates and colleagues in Iran: (from L to R) Mr Shahryar, Mr Zulfiqari, Mr Rajawar, Mr Bedi, Mrs Rajawar, Mr BV Agarwal, Mrs Shahryar, Mr TV Lonan, Mrs Lonan, Mr Disa, Mrs D'Souza, Captain D'Souza, Mrs Disa, Mr Bagheri, Mr Akbari, Mr Amini and Mr Dutta

Below: With associates at a dinner party in Tehran: (from L to R) The author, Mr Souri, Chairman, IRISL, Mr Khalili, the Indian Ambassador, my wife Manju, Mrs Rajawar, Admiral Gandhi, Chairman, SCI, Mr R Zade, Mr Zeineddin, and Mr Rajawar (from whom I took over the post of Managing Director of Irano-Hind)

Above: The children had some good times in Tehran before the Iranian Revolution, when they were sent back to India because all English-medium schools in Iran were closed after the Revolution

Below: My mother Amer Devi Mehrotra and I at my office in Mumbai, 1986

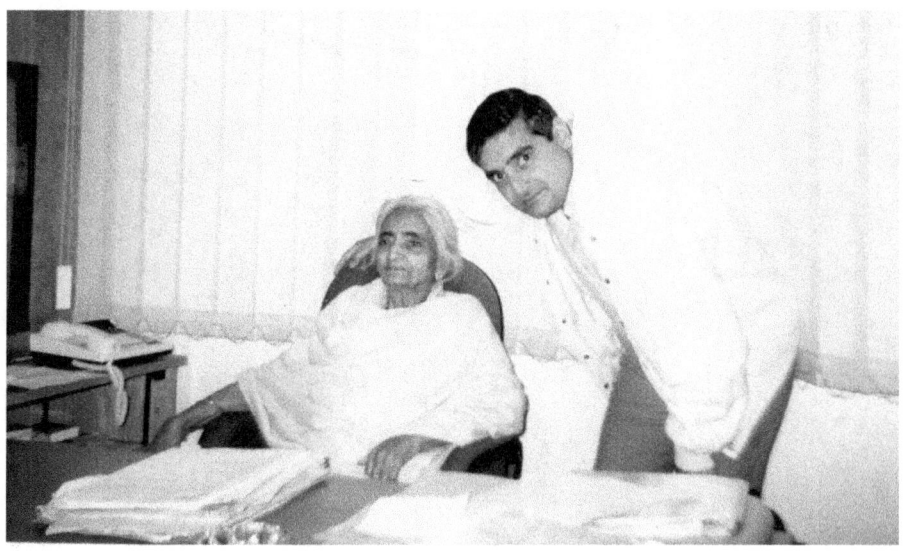

Above: Our pre-Revolution home at Zargandeh, Tehran, Iran

Below: Our post-Revolution home in Tehran on the 11th floor of the third building from the left

Life Lesson Eight

Opportunity and entrepreneurship both nurture creative thinking and innovation, and that's impossible without people who have the talent to think outside the box.

ESCAPE YOUR BOX

Every day, you'll have opportunities to take chances and to work outside your safety net. Sure, it's a lot easier to stay in your comfort zone... in my case, business suits and real estate... but sometimes you have to take risks. When the risks pay off, that's when you reap the biggest rewards.

Donald Trump

Whether we realise it or not, life has many wonderful opportunities, but we have to be open to possibilities. I have always wondered why we limit these possibilities by confining ourselves to our box – our comfort zone. Reaching for things outside our box is uncomfortable and sometimes frightening. But if you have ambition, as I had, the cramped space will eventually leave you frustrated and depressed. Ask yourself what the limits of your box are, and whether it fits your mental picture of who you want to be or where you want to go? If you're living in a way that is limiting you, get outside your box and learn something new which requires you to stretch beyond your comfort zone and challenges you. Make sure it will move you closer to becoming the person you'd like to be, or doing the things you'd love to do. Step boldly outside your box, so that you can receive all that is available to you and achieve your ambitions. Stepping out of my box was leaving a secure and well-paid job and starting out on my own, to make my dreams and ambitions a reality and identifying, along the way, key people to help me build my dream. I have learnt, during my experiences, that entrepreneurship produces solutions that challenge the status quo and involve risk-taking and the pursuit of opportunities that others may fail to recognise, or may even view as problems or threats; it is closely associated with change, creativity, knowledge, innovation and flexibility, and is impossible to achieve without the right people. Once the right people are in place, the next step is to maintain and retain those valuable resources – keeping employee satisfaction high, making work meaningful, and rewarding people for co-operative and collaborative efforts.

During my five-year tenure as Principal Advisor on Shipping in Iran, I had developed the image in the international shipping industry of a hardworking and thorough professional. My solid reputation and good relations with several international shipping associates provided the base upon which I grew my Company. These associates had already arranged all clearances required from the UK government to form a company owned solely and entirely by me. This saw the registration of Foresight Limited in London on 4 September 1984 as the financial and administrative centre, with me as the sole owner but with hardly any capital for we started with very little. We used our savings, and we even sublet the (second-hand) photocopier – anything to save or generate cash, as we gradually created business, cashflow and, eventually, profit.

I began to draw up the blueprints of my new life, with the children safely at school in London. Simultaneously, we opened Inter Shipping and Trading in Zurich (recommended to me as the heart of the banking world and where I hoped to gain access to the banks from which we badly needed funds) to manage the operational side of things. I shuttled back and forth for quite a few years, but eventually my lack of proficiency in German got the better of me and we closed it.

Cherish your visions and your dreams, as they are the children of your soul; the blueprints of your ultimate achievements.
Napoleon Hill

The experience of dealing with all the ups and downs in the shipping industry and setting up the joint venture company during the last nine years in Iran had provided me with the confidence that I would be more than able to make my own venture a success. For some time, I am sure that even my wife felt as the rest of the family believed – that I had gone crazy and quit a career that was on the upswing in order to try my hand at entrepreneurship, without a substantial capital base of my own. We all knew that in the shipping world one needed millions of dollars to buy ships. I persuaded my wife to give me two years to see if I could fulfil my ambition to become a ship owner. She agreed, supportive as always, and God has been merciful and benevolent.

My first employee was Claire Horsley, an alumnus of London Business School, and a very close friend. Nezam Zeineddin, my deputy from my stint as Principal Advisor on Shipping, also joined me in London but, with a family to support, the lack of funds bothered him – he was not as adventurous and fond of risks as I was – so I arranged for him to work with a firm in Sweden. He later moved to DNV and is now working with them in Canada. A few more of my treasured associates from my Irano Hind days also joined me in my new venture – first Flavian D'Souza, then Anil Deshpande, and S.K. Datta, who retired some years later. They have been with me ever since. Subsequently we were joined by Philippa Wright, who came to us from the NHS, and is still with us today and G.Venkat, who took up where S.K. Datta left off and then R.T. Sreenivasa, who took over from him.

Keep good company. Keep a brain trust of people you can call on in tough times in dark hours. Share your dreams!
David Heenan

We also enjoyed the invaluable contributions of Paul Willcox and Claire Horsley, who have been close friends and associates for a very long time. Paul recently recalled that he first met me at Gothenburg airport on the way to Helsinki, when I had just taken over as Managing Director of Irano Hind Shipping from Mr L.M.S. Rajawar. He remembers that I plied him with questions about reefer ships throughout the trip, something he was not familiar with at the time, and that I faced down the full force of the Finnish ship owners in Helsinki who had supplied us four bulk carriers, one of which was not as per contract (the matter went to arbitration and the verdict went in Irano Hind's favour a year or so later).

Paul became a regular visitor to Tehran, helping me to acquire reefer ships for Irano Hind, and we often hosted him at our home where he was regaled with refreshments usually not available in the Islamic Republic of Iran. At the weekends there were always pleasant walks up into the mountains. It was he whom I quizzed about the practicalities of moving to London and setting up a new venture there. When we finally made the move in 1984, Claire and he both did their best to ease Manju, the children and I into our new surroundings. They helped us find a flat near their own home in Islington, and Manju was quite happy shopping in Chapel Street Market. When Saurabh and Manjari found places in schools in South West London, they helped us with our move to Putney and we have lived there ever since.

We were frequent visitors at Paul's parents' house in Surrey, and I loved the long, peaceful country walks, pushing Claire and Paul's daughter Alexandra, aged two, in her buggy. Paul taught me to jog on one of our morning walks, and on another he introduced me to the fruits of the hedgerow, which I still relish. I also learnt the hard way to be cautious: my looks and sounds of disgust when I bit into a shiny conker remain fixed in their minds! Paul helped me out when I was setting up Foresight in many ways, not least by subletting me office space in Rodwell House, from which to start my business, and supported me in every possible way. The office began with some very old furniture (some of which we still own today), a couple of phones, a telex machine, and a drinks machine to keep me company. Claire, whom I had requested to help me out a little in the office, walked in on a Tuesday afternoon to see what she could do to help, and stayed with us for the next sixteen years, handling all our legal affairs and liaising with banks. The small set-up soon grew to smart new offices in the same building, which I also sublet from Paul.

Paul and Claire continued to advise me on important issues like the choice of car – it was they who informed me that the well-heeled Englishman prefers a Jaguar to a Mercedes, and helped me to buy my first XJ saloon second-hand, from a dealer who parted with it for half of what it was worth. Since then, I have continued to buy Jaguars, though now they are new off the assembly line.

Foresight Limited began as a small company, struggling to meet both ends by doing small shipping errand jobs, such as barter deals with the Islamic Republic of Iran, based on my high-level contacts from my Iran days. Those were deals in which Iran paid in oil, the price of which was low and the product in surplus, rather than foreign exchange, of which they had very little. Though I knew that these barter deals would not mature or show any cashflow until more than a year had passed, I took them on to ensure us at least a little cash in the short term. In fact, with our savings rapidly diminishing, our very first job was ship broking for the Iranians, which yielded 1.25 per cent commission on the value of each deal.

Two years after I began my company, I bought my first ship, a multipurpose, container-oriented tween-decker in the beginning of 1986, *Amer Kanti* (built in 1979), named after my sister Kanti, who passed away in 1972. The prefix *Amer*, as I have mentioned earlier, was derived from my mother's name – Amer Devi. Simultaneously I established Amer Ship Management Limited (ASM) in Mumbai in 1986, to undertake technical management and crewing of the Foresight vessels, and then began undertaking third-party management of vessels. We also bought another multi-purpose container-oriented tween-decker in 1987, called *Amer Asha*, named after my mother-in-law. With broking fees earning us US$4m annually by 1988, we shifted our focus more and more to our own fleet, but it was ship broking which gave us that much-needed filip which moved us from a struggling start-up to a flourishing business.

> *Twenty years from now you will be more disappointed by the things that you didn't do than by the ones you did do. So throw off the bowlines. Sail away from the safe harbour. Catch the trade winds in your sails. Explore. Dream. Discover.*
> Mark Twain

Suddenly, like a bolt out of the blue, my past caught up with me to sweep me onwards atop a wave of success. Iran and Iraq had been fighting a war since September 1980. In 1984 the French Government sold Exocet missiles to Iraq, which had a short-range and a low TNT value (69 kg), but were effective in immobilising ships by implosion. Iraq intensified its attacks and began to aim at crude oil tankers that were coming to Iran's Kharg Island to buy oil. The Iranians could intercept Iraqi fighter and bombers but not the Exocet missiles, and the result was that Iranian exports suffered miserably and their ships' war insurance skyrocketed. In addition, they needed to rapidly expand their owned fleet through the purchase of second-hand vessels and, in 1985, Mr Souri (formerly of IRISL and now with NITC) and the Iranian Government contacted me and asked me to return to Iran to handle the situation, treating it as an emergency. I stipulated that if they wanted my expertise, they would have to hire my company, Foresight Limited.

Our belief at the beginning of a doubtful undertaking is the one thing that assures the successful outcome of any venture.
William James

Iran agreed, and appointed Foresight Limited to handle the crisis. We abandoned the barter deals halfway through and switched to the unique and extremely profitable opportunity of creating the world's first tanker shuttle service, by creating a floating terminal for oil export from Iran, outside the Gulf, and to charter thirty very large crude carriers (VLCCs) to shuttle over three million barrels of oil per day between Kharg Island and the floating terminal from where the international buyers bought the oil from Iran. It was then that Foresight Limited bought its first VLCCs, *Trade Reliance*, in 1987 and *Valiant Carrier*, in 1988. I still consider this my finest professional achievement. Within six months of its inception, our small London-based shipping company became a world-renowned oil transporter and exporter. In over four hundred trips in three years that the VLCC shuttles made from Kharg Island to the floating terminal, they were hit only eight percent of the time. And in all that time only two lives were lost.

The other detail we had to worry about was the war insurance on Iranian ships. The value of the premium was dependent on the value of the ship, and the risk was worked out by the probability of the ship being hit within the fifteen days of insurance cover. Lloyds of London was at that time offering cover at almost half the value of the ship. I appreciated that, if we went without insurance cover, the losses would be catastrophic yet, at the going rates, insuring our ships and those we had chartered from various owners would also put us in the red. Trapped in this seemingly impossible situation, my team and I did some innovative thinking. We studied both ends of the situation and we came up with the idea of floating a twenty-two percent war cover policy through the Bimeh Iran (National Insurance Company of Iran), at their London office. Foresight became its representative for shipping companies. Policies were issued in the United Kingdom, in view of the political risk perceived for Iran, guaranteed by one hundred million US dollars that the Central Bank of Iran placed in their Bank Melli branch in London. It covered catastrophe, excess of loss, and risk excess of our franchise. Foresight Limited managed its papers and all the follow-up. Today, this is a policy that has acquired the dubious status of being the world's most famous war insurance and, by the end of the war, Bimeh Iran had made a profit of three million US dollars, while still managing to keep its guarantee seed fund of one hundred million intact.

> *You do things when the opportunities come along. I've had periods in my life when I've had a bundle of ideas come along, and I've had long dry spells. If I get an idea next week, I'll do something. If not, I won't do a damn thing.*
> Warren Buffett

My initial business was and remains shipping, but my exposure to oil trading during the Iran-Iraq War and running the shuttle service gave me a comfortable feeling for the oil sector, and that is how, after the end of the war in 1989, I decided to diversify into oil drilling to ensure that my relationship with the National Iranian Oil Company continued.

In 1989 the office of Amer Shipping Limited was opened in Nicosia, Cyprus. The year also marked the commissioning of two more refrigerated ships from the Toyohashi shipyard in Japan. In March 1990, the first ship – *Amer Himalaya* – embarked on her maiden voyage, and in November of the same year, the second – *Amer Fuji* – was launched.

When we joined the shipbuilders to celebrate delivery of the ships in Japan, we were treated to a fine meal of sushi, the raw fish dish acknowledged internationally as one of the delicacies of Japanese cuisine. A guest and associate of mine, Mr Amini Nejad from Tehran, would have none of it, and began to barbecue his sushi over a candle. Watching this, Paul Willcox whispered 'Three thousand years of civilisation goes up in smoke!'

By 1990, the Iraq-Kuwait war had begun. The United States of America had intervened and the American bias in favour of Kuwait was clear. For the first time in history, the US decided to charter ships from its allied countries to carry out the ferrying of ammunition, supplies, Minutemen, missiles and war gear to and fro. I saw the tremendous potential and approached the people concerned. Foresight was seen as a perfect fit. Our ships were hired and the stamp of approval of the United States of America on our chartering expertise did much to lift our image in the international scene, associated as we were primarily with the Persian Gulf. This particular venture ended with the end of the war in 1995, but left us with a firm foundation and reputation for Foresight, a thirst for expansion into reefer shipping and the purchase of more ships. We had also stolen a march on the competition.

> *Belief in oneself is one of the most important bricks in building*
> *any successful venture.*
> Lydia M Child

In 1989, we established a drilling activities cell – Foresight Drilling. Soon after that, *Foresight Driller II* (a deep water drill ship) and *Foresight Driller III* (a three hundred foot water depth jack up rig) were acquired. Our first drilling contract was signed with the National Iranian Oil Corporation (NIOC) to develop the Sirri oil fields. At the same time, we bid for *Foresight Driller II* to work with the Oil and Natural Gas Company (ONGC) of India on offshore exploration in India, but the deal never went through, due to objections raised in the Indian courts by vessels flying Indian flags. In 1991, *Foresight Driller III*, freshly refitted in

Singapore, began work on the NIOC contract in Iran, and was engaged in wellhead maintenance – she finished the contract successfully, was sent to be upgraded in Sharjah, and then mobilised for India, where ONGC had contracted us to develop various areas of Mumbai High oilfields. *Foresight Driller II*, sadly, was under-employed, due to unsatisfactory developments with ONGC and a consequent fall in the drill ship market worldwide. She had to be sold in 1995 at a considerable loss, and I was extremely unhappy about it.

Ten years into the life of Foresight Limited, things were looking better and better. By this time, we owned more than fifteen ships, and were looking for more funds to service more dreams. Like all our other ventures, our foray into the hospitality sector too was under unusual circumstances. In 1991, the then Mayor of Shanghai, whom I had met at a shipping conference in Shanghai, invited me to open the city's first Indian restaurant. I was, of course, a bit taken aback, since we had no prior experience in the hospitality field and it was literally an uncharted ocean for us. Like everything else, I took it as a challenge, establishing the hospitality division in November 1992. The first restaurant, *The Tandoor*, opened in the Jin Jiang Hotel in Shanghai in October 1994.

From 1992 to 1997, our reefer business flourished. We had excellent charters with Cool Carriers of Sweden and CSAV of Chile, and the cashflow for the business was reasonably good. Foresight Drilling was the first company in India to handle Horizontal Oil Drilling for the Indian Oil and Natural Gas Company (ONGC) and worked with them for five-and-a-half years from 1993 to 1997. Our tankers *Amer Energy* and *Amer Power* were regularly employed and we had begun to profit from their operations too.

Meanwhile, Foresight Drilling was going flat out. *Foresight Driller III* had successfully completed her ONGC contract, and was then sold to Foramar France in 1997. *Foresight Driller V* (a light jack up rig, formerly called *Odin Moon*) was bought in 1998, and was soon profitably employed.

My personal life too was filled with happiness. Both my son and daughter were wed within a year of each other – Manjari to Utsav in 1997, and Saurabh to Neha in 1998. Like any entrepreneurial father, I had given (or tried to give) my son Saurabh a good education and, during his BSc (a four year co-op course) at Brunel University near London, he worked six months each year (as part of the course) at a different company. He began with Lloyds (insurance) of London the first year, followed in consecutive years by a tenure as a cadet on a ship, followed by another with the refrigerated transportation specialists Cool Carriers in Stockholm; then he did a stint with a shipping bank, and finished up with six months at Pari-Bas Bank in Geneva. To prepare for his MSc in Shipping and Trade Finance at City University, and to gain the requisite additional year of experience, he worked at a boutique shipping bank in London. He then completed his MSc and worked with my company Foresight for a year or two before taking a sabbatical and working with other companies, in order to try his wings as a young man in a hurry who wanted to make his mark on the world. He is now back with Foresight, having gained valuable experience that he is putting to good use with the company.

> *Whatever they grow up to be, they are still our children, and the one most important of all the things we can give to them is unconditional love. Not a love that depends on anything at all except that they are our children.*
> Rosaleen Dickson

My daughter Manjari's marriage to Utsav Seth, son of Mr Guru Seth of Agra, India, unexpectedly brought yet another venture into my life. Mr Guru Seth owned a shoe component manufacturing plant in Puducheri in South India, catering to the growing shoe export market in south India. After the wedding, I wanted Utsav to join the Foresight group to learn the business of shipping, oil drilling and exploration, so that both my son and my son-in-law would be on an equal footing within my business, and their relationship would always be smooth sailing in the long term. But my son-in-law Utsav declined, saying that he loved the shoe business and, if his father-in-law chose to invest, he would welcome the assistance. I honoured his wishes, and told him that it would not be an issue with me.

If the mountain will not come to Mohammed, then Mohammed
must go to the mountain.
Proverb

At that point, I was fifty-seven years old, and decided to learn about this new business. I went to the Puducheri factory and studied the process, and then decided to persuade Utsav's father Mr Guru Seth, now we were related, to let me take over the Puducheri factory. He did so reluctantly, on the condition that he retained his shares in the Company. I agreed, and undertook that as someone formerly involved only in shipping, oil drilling and exploration, I would henceforth invest time, effort and finances to make the shoe component factory prosper and achieve international renown. Thus it was that in 1999, GTFC – I did not change the original name, keeping my promise to Mr Seth – became a part of Foresight's portfolio.

It is to Utsav's credit that, within two years of these events, the Company had captured nearly half the Indian shoe component market, whereas our nearest competitor had only eight percent. However, we realised that, because shoe components represent only ten percent of the value of the entire shoe, no matter what we did, the maximum turnover that we could achieve was ten million US dollars a year. Compared to the shipping and oil drilling branches of our businesses, this section would always remain small. My 'antennae' began to twitch, and I started sending out feelers, seeking solutions that might expand the enterprise's potential, among them an option in the information technology sector, which did not work out. I decided to ask Utsav to move to London, so that he could network with shoe importers in Europe. His second-in-command, B. Nanban, took over operations in India. This resulted in the conception of another venture – The Shoe Club Limited at the end of 2004 – an international supply chain management business, to enable European retailers and wholesalers to source high quality leather shoes from India and the rest of Asia. That became highly successful in a very short time.

It is not what we get, but who we become, what we contribute...
that gives meaning to our lives.
Anthony Robbins

While these events were unfolding and my Company was slowly turning into an empire, I felt that, having received so much, I should also give back to the country of my birth and the community from which I rose. Though living in London, I considered Kanpur my home town, and felt that, whatever I started, be it a charity or an institution, it should be based there. While I was in Mumbai on an official trip in June 1998, I and a few of my Captains decided that my philanthropy should take the shape of a maritime training institute. Such institutes were thus far restricted to coastal regions or the capital at Delhi. My institute would be the first to have the backing of a reputable shipping company and be located somewhere other than Mumbai.

The house in which I was born and which my father had built with his savings was to be the location, a team was sent to Kanpur in June 1999, and Mr R.S. Nayar, a consultant of repute, presented me with a project report in July 1999. On 15 May 2001, a local team, headed by my late brother's wife, Mrs Bina Mehrotra, and a Master Mariner, Captain Yogesh Bhanti, was raised to oversee proceedings and the development of the academy training programme. The work of conversion was begun, and a small part of the original house kept as offices. As I had done with my ships, I dedicated the institute to the memory of my beloved mother and called it the Amer Maritime Training Academy (AMTA), arranging for it to be a registered charity under the Amer Ship Owners and Rig Owners Association, Mumbai. The team succeeded in getting the Academy approved by the Directorate General of Shipping of the Government of India in 2002. In May 2002, AMTA also received approval from them to conduct four basic *Standards of Training, Certification & Watchkeeping '95* modular courses on their behalf – *Elementary First Aid, Personal Survival Techniques, Fire Prevention & Fire Fighting and Personal Safety and Social Responsibility.* AMTA conducted the first of the four courses in June 2002.

It is every man's obligation to put back into the world at least the
equivalent of what he takes out of it.
Albert Einstein

I formally inaugurated the institute on 8 December 2002, with a press conference. Bearing in mind the general standard of fluency in English, a *Maritime English* course was also designed to begin in May 2003, to accustom the cadets to working on board ships crewed by a variety of nationalities. I also decided to enhance the uniqueness of the institute by assuring graduate placements on Foresight vessels. Candidates started to flood in from all over the state and from other parts of India as well. The school has never looked back. Nothing gives one quite the level of happiness and satisfaction as being able to help so many young people and, most of all, the chance to return something to one's homeland. I follow their progress keenly, and return there periodically to speak to the students. In 2008, AMTA also began an *Oil Rig Operation Familiarisation* course for students who wanted to begin their career as crew aboard rigs. This course was also approved by the Directorate General of Hydrocarbons of the Government of India, and is the first of its kind in India.

From employee to entrepreneur, I had moved in to a new arena. Modest beginnings had, with the help of dedicated colleagues, to a decade of success, from barter deals to contracts, from ships to oil rigs. We had diversified into the hospitality trade too, and then the footwear industry.

I had escaped from my box.

Above: In Amsterdam in the 1980s

Above (l to r): Paul and Claire

Below (l to r): Anil, Flavian and Philippa

Facing page: Two of the first ships I bought, their names prefixed, as all my ships were, by my mother's name 'Amer': *Amer Kanti*, named for my sister Kanti who passed away at a young age; *Amer Asha*, named for my mother-in-law Asha Tandon (Photographs © FotoFlite www. fotoflite.com)

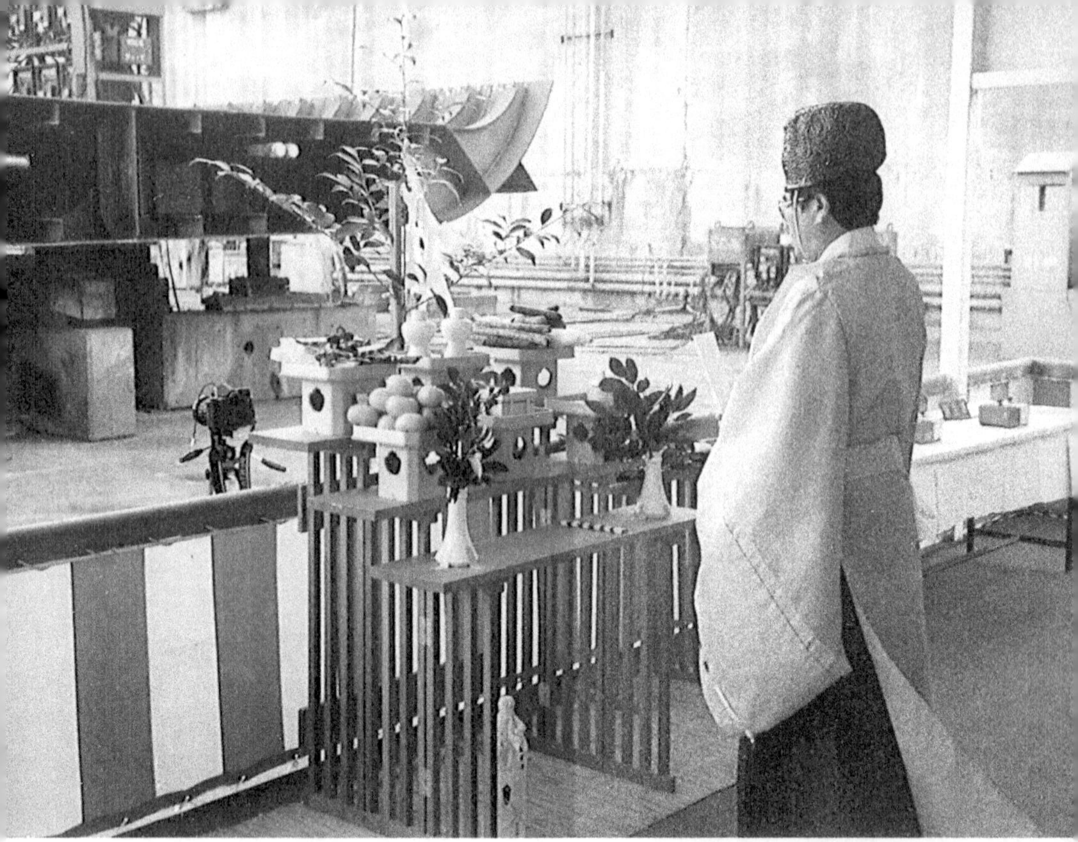

Above: The keel-laying ceremony for *Amer Himalaya* in November 1989 at the Japanese shipyard where I had ordered two new ships

Below: The launch of one of the ships newly built for us in Japan – *Amer Himalaya*

Right: The other ship built for us in Japan – *Amer Fuji* – was launched in November 2000 (Photograph © FotoFlite www.fotoflite.com)

Above: I've always kept in touch with my roots as a marine engineer... here I am on a visit to our oil rig *Foresight Driller III*

Below: Another of my rigs, *Foresight Driller V*

Above: I formally inaugurated the Amer Maritime Training Institute in Kanpur on 8th December 2002

Centre: A report on the feasibility of setting up a Marine Training Institute in my hometown of Kanpur was presented to me in July 1999 by Mr RS Nayar

Below: On the steps of the Elder Street offices of Foresight Limited in London

Life Lesson Nine

Financing your dream is tough, and tougher still is saving your dream when it becomes a nightmare.

MAKE FAILURE WORK

Never give in! Never give in, never, never, never never.

Winston Churchill

Every successful and enduring company passes through times of success and times of imminent failure. My Company is no exception. During the times of near-failure, most business owners and managers forget there is no magic switch or one key element that will restore their business to health overnight – just as pain and suffering are hidden in our lives, failure is inherent in all our actions and undertakings. The good thing about failure is that it is temporary, manageable and solvable. Anticipate what kind of failures you may expect on the way and prepare yourself adequately to cope with them – batten down the hatches, and develop alternative scenarios to deal with issues that may develop from time to time and interfere with your progress, in order to minimise losses, conserve resources and remain focused on goals. Consider failure as a phase in the process of improvement and development and use it for self-improvement and increased self-awareness. Cultivate equanimity of mind to cope with both success and failure with the same mindset. Weak people are easily disheartened and admit failure, but strong-willed people are determined to end failure, through actions borne out of analysis and observation and sustained by the will to persevere. When faced with failure, a strong-willed person continues on his chosen path, secure in the knowledge that defeat lies not in failure, but in his own fears and so-called limitations; he has the freedom and the opportunity to try different options and alternative methods to deal with and resolve failure. A strong-willed person does not give up, would not leave in between, would not abandon the hope of success and would not lose sight of the resources that he has invested in the pursuit of success.

Nobody expects an empire of any kind to be set up and sustained without any low points. But sometimes the lows can be of such depth that they threaten the very life of the empire you have so painstakingly built up. All my life I have gone about dreaming dreams that seemed as outlandish to others as they sometimes seemed to me. Nevertheless, I went about systematically translating those dreams into reality. Financing your dreams is the tough part, especially if you begin without any capital of your own. More difficult than that is to bring the dream back to life after it has started to turn into a nightmare. And yet more difficult by far is trying to save and preserve your energy to nurse the creation which was the result of your dream.

> *Nothing splendid has ever been achieved except by those who*
> *dared believe that something inside of them was superior to*
> *circumstances.*
> Bruce Barton

It had all begun in 1997, when we were looking for financing to buy more ships and fund our existing refrigerated ship operations in order to become significant players in the world's reefer business. Our reefer management division was in trouble through lack of capacity. We needed more ships – we only had four and, since it was our core expertise, we wanted it to be one of our best divisions. Nevertheless, money was tight, and the division needed an urgent injection of funds. Added to that, the small chemical tankers we had bought were not finding employment, even in the traditionally low-end market of the Far East, transporting palm oil to India. Yet we had to keep pouring money in to keep them maintained in a decent condition. The options open to us in the market at the time were the Norwegian banks, an IPO (initial public offering of shares) in the Indian private equity market for oil drilling or the USA bond market. By the mid-1990s American High Yield Bonds had become so ubiquitous that they seemed to be the best option for our needs. Speculative, non-investment-grade instruments, or junk bonds as they are known, rated below investment grade at the time of purchase, with a higher risk of default, typically pay higher yields than better quality bonds, making them attractive to risk-taking investors – and appealing to those in search of ready finance. Shipping is a risky business, and banks do not lend on the same basis as junk bonds, redeemed on maturity (after ten years) by one bullet payment of the full amount.

Hindsight is of little value in the decision-making process.
It distorts our memory for events that occurred at the time of the
decision so that the actual consequence seems to have
been a 'foregone conclusion'. Thus, it may be difficult to
learn from our mistakes.
Diane F. Halpern

In hindsight (the direct opposite to my Company's name), I wonder whether I would have taken this option had I even the tiniest inkling of what was in the future. Extensive and exhaustive preparations were required before we could even attempt to showcase our Company to potential investors in the American equity and bond market – we had to produce accurate and detailed financial records for the past decade and found an ideal partner in the New York-based Donaldson, Lufkin & Jenrette (DLJ), an investment bank dealing in a variety of services. They had forewarned us that the investors we were seeking would be in the high yield capital market, since the shipping industry was treated as a high risk business. DLJ did the requisite hand-holding while we prepared our presentations, slides and speeches to market our proposals. Anil Deshpande, G. Venkat, Michael Revell and I, after much practice, managed to make the cultural crossover required to be successful in raising money from US investors. It took us sixteen dry runs before DLJ were satisfied that we were ready to go head to head against other companies seeking financing in the same sector.

Unity is strength... when there is teamwork and collaboration,
wonderful things can be achieved.
Mattie Stepanek

We hired a nine-seater private jet, covered seventeen cities in eleven days, and had a total of thirty-two meetings in two weeks with potential investors. It was an unusual experience for Anil, Michael, Venkat and me, dressed in our best business suits. We gave presentations to financiers from Merrill Lynch and the like who, casually dressed in jeans and tee-shirts, had an attention span of a mere thirty minutes, skipped the pleasantries and cut straight to the chase. It was an effort to make the jump from their informal appearance to the fact that a seemingly casual attitude did not reflect their business acumen or financial worth. They had already read our dossiers. All they came to see were the people behind the proposal and to assess our capabilities. At the end of the meetings, we had found our money. As always, there were other issues that cropped up. DLJ had led us to believe that the money would come at a cheaper rate of interest than the investors were asking – it was expensive money! It made us hesitate, but the decision had to be made quickly or we would lose out to our competitors, and I would have to start from scratch in Europe or Asia with no certainty of success. We decided to take the risk – after all, we had already spent six million US dollars and precious time and effort in order to raise the one hundred million US dollars we were being offered, as secured finance with a ten-year bullet payment.

Risks must be taken, because the greatest
hazard in life is to risk nothing.
Leo F. Buscaglia

With the paperwork completed, the bonds were issued to the investors, mostly from the United States of America and some in Europe. When we received the money, we financed the purchase of three more reefer ships that we had wanted to add to our portfolio, and planned the upgrade of our reefer management division. We made a strategic decision to consolidate all our shipping services under one roof and so moved the reefers from Mumbai, India, to Nicosia, Cyprus by May 1999. The tankers remained in Mumbai. The ships' technical management was easier now because all our reefers were run under one roof, and we now had a base of competent staff and technical talent in place, under the leadership of Anil Deshpande, who agreed to move to Cyprus as MD.

As a result of the bond issue, the reefer business increased and we created Amer Reefer Company (ARC) in November 1997, but our tankers were becoming more and more expensive to maintain and their profitability was dropping rapidly. Soon, a similar fate hit the entire shipping industry and, by early 2000, the reefer market began a cyclical downturn. Once again, we were in familiar terrain – hard pressed for cash. Like most of our competitors we were looking for cargo to transport but, with the agonising financial rider of paying back the interest to the holders of the bonds, which had begun to trade at lower than their par value. ARC was in deep trouble and on the brink of bankruptcy. By the middle of 2000, I could see the writing on the wall. It was clear that we were facing a breach of covenant. Most of all, I did not want to lose my ships to banks or creditors, or in the manner in which I had to sell my drill ship (*Foresight Driller II*) in 1995.

I began talks with our advisory bank, Chase Securities, informing them that I had insufficient funds to pay the interest to the bondholders and that our future earnings were also uncertain, since the market was in a rapid decline. Strangely enough, they made our inability to pay up sound like a virtue. Chase Securities contended that we could file for Chapter Eleven of the United States Business Law provision – an attempt to stay in business while a bankruptcy court supervised the reorganisation of the Company's contractual and debt obligations, then granted partial or complete relief from most of the debts and contracts so the Company could make a fresh start. This modern halfway house was designed to protect the employees of basically sound companies in temporary, but potentially terminal difficulties

Most of the important things in the world have been accomplished by people who have kept on trying when there seemed to be no hope at all.
Dale Carnegie

Chase Securities said this should convince bondholders they were better off accepting twenty or thirty cents per original dollar invested, rather than losing more and not getting any interest from loss-making assets. They would also help us file the Chapter Eleven claim and, either having got the courts to approve our reorganisation plan, or reaching a settlement with the majority of the bondholders, find us fresh finance. Of course, not everything goes as well as it should. Our creditors and bondholders, who wanted to wrest control of the assets, claimed our incompetence in the Chapter 11 proceedings, in the hope that the courts would find in their favour, resulting in the termination of rights and interests of the Company's stockholders, and transference of ownership of the assets and a reorganised Company to the creditors. Vulture funds smelt an opportunity to buy low and sell high, and began to acquire our bonds from restless investors, calculating that the Company's plans would fail and they would wrest control of our assets. If we were to hold on to our Company and our assets, we had to prove that Amer Reefer Company was a victim of unforeseen market forces and not of gross mismanagement. This was difficult, since the majority of the bonds were held by predatory funds and owners, who wanted to take control away from us.

I could at this point see a long drawn-out battle awaiting me. Rather than paying attention to the business, which was in dire straits, my most productive people would have all their energy consumed by this process. Our preparations with Chase Securities began in early summer in 2000. The agreement that they drew up for us was too far in their favour and we came up with a counter-offer which was to share the outcome of any agreement struck with creditors and to link up Chase's fee with the exit-price that Amer Reefer Company would get on a successful conclusion of the Chapter Eleven proceedings. Anil used his usual persuasive skills and, after some hesitation, Chase agreed to this, and a final mandate was signed. As it turned out, this agreement saved us the draining away of our already dwindling resources by deferring the Bank's fees. We next found lawyers in the United States of America to file the claim for us – Cadwalader, Wickersham and Taft LLP – who had a track record of never having lost a single Chapter Eleven claim. This in itself was perhaps the turning point. At first the lawyers literally laughed us out of court. They were accustomed to dealing with cases in the billions of dollars. Ours was enormous to us, but petty cash to them, unlikely to yield the multi-million dollar fees which fired their boilers. They declined.

It is at times like these that the instinct, will and, frankly, fury at what looks irrational and unnecessary combine to bring the best out of people or sometimes the very worst. I looked at their record, and realised they had no traction in the maritime field, high risk that it is, yet with cycles like the one we faced, which ultimately yield financial upheavals and corporate disruption on a global scale – and the opportunities for very respectable legal fees. So I went back to them. I told them that, if they saved us, they would have a new market and a headstart. They might not make much out of me, but they would assuredly profit in the long term from other, future, major cases. They saw the light. And they took us on.

The claim was officially filed by 12 March 2001. Between then and September, we put our reorganisation plans in place. Anil and Raphael worked tirelessly to produce all the relevant accounting records and prepare our financial and commercial case, in itself an onerous task. Everything seemed to be going according to plan as the Chapter 11 process unfolded.

If things go wrong, don't go with them.
Roger Ward Babson

Yet another ugly turn of events was waiting in the shadows to swoop down upon our unsuspecting heads. Just before the 9/11 attacks, we received some devastating news – Dutch shipping tycoon Coco Vroon and Aston Financial International (AFI), a company associated with Norwegian rig and ship-owner Kristian Siem, had made a joint purchase of close to sixty-six percent of Amer Shipping Company bonds, and were making a bid to buy us out. Another minute percentage would allow them enough voting rights to foil our entire reorganisation plan and take control of the Company and our ships. Anil made an urgent trip to Stockholm and Copenhagen to talk to Lauritzen Cool and convince bondholder Tom Mackay to sell his small deciding share to us to avoid a Vroom and AFI shareholder majority. We were bidding with empty pockets so, when our charterers Lauritzen Cool were unable to provide us with a short-term facility, we lost Mackay's bonds to Vroon and AFI, controlled by Christian Siem, whose joint holding was now the majority and that left us with less than twenty percent.

When a ship begins to sink, a great many parts fall apart in the process – some of our key staff resigned, and Coco Vroon was also clearly sending signals to our remaining staff to switch loyalties. As if this was not enough trouble to handle, Chase Securities was bought out by JP Morgan, and they withdrew the promise of financing us after the Chapter Eleven proceedings. The only redemption was that our signed mandate saved us from paying them any fees at all. By the middle of 2002, we needed to look for a new financier for our reorganisation plan because, unless we found one, we would not be able to convince the courts that our plan was valid. Even if we did manage to find a financier, Vroon and AFI could still vote us out with their majority holding in my own Company. We searched and sought, and finally found, a willing source of funds. Nordea Bank agreed to back us if we came out of Chapter Eleven proceedings clean and in one piece.

Now we faced Chapter 11 proceedings. We flew to New York, where our lawyers, Gregory Petrick and Barry Seidel, faced Judge Arthur J. Gonzalez. That morning the Court sat for the final session and our man addressed the Judge. Everything he said was correct; all the evidence pointed to our competence, the cyclical nature of difficulties beyond our control, the iniquities of the bond system, and the predatory nature of our competitors. The Judge was impartial and unimpressed. This was just another case where the business had come unstuck, by using standard means of finance, hitting a bad patch, and finding itself unable to meet its obligations, albeit to some fairly dubious speculators. There really wasn't a case for stepping in. We would go down. Then counsellor paused, looked the Judge in the eye and said that, without Chapter 11 protection, our employees would suffer. The Judge didn't blink. Counsellor added that wages, prices, services would suffer. The Judge seemed unsurprised. Our man then commented, almost casually it seemed, that of course, as things stood, Vroon's outfit would acquire our assets and our customers because, without us, there would be no competition. The Judge sat up. Our man continued. If Vroon took over, we would be dismembered, there would be fewer ships, fewer jobs, fewer staff, higher prices – no competition. That was it. The Judge ruled. We had three months to do a deal with Vroon. If there was no compromise, he would decide for us. If we succeeded, we could carry on.

> *Imaginary obstacles are insurmountable. Real ones aren't.*
> *But you can't tell the difference when you have no real*
> *information. Fear can create even more imaginary obstacles than*
> *ignorance can. That's why the smallest step away from speculation*
> *and into reality can be an amazing relief.*
> *The Reality Solution means: Do it before you're ready.*
> Barbara Sher

In trying to get Vroon and AFI into negotiations, we reasoned with them to arrive at a mutual settlement, rather than using all our joint and several resources, time and energy in suiting someone else's purpose. There were many details involved in the negotiations, but fortunately for us, we were able to agree that, at the end of it, we would buy back the bonds from them, albeit at a much higher price than they had acquired them, giving them a profit of over twenty percent. We had the advantage of full ownership of the ships and of buying back the bonds at less cost than otherwise, saving accrued and unpaid interest. Finally, on 17 October 2002, ARC emerged from US Chapter Eleven bankruptcy protection, after we completed the restructuring of its junk bond issue, and returned to the purely private fold after an unhappy five-year relationship with the public capital markets. That evening, Anil Deshpande, G. Venkat, Philippa Wright and I were in New York, too exhausted to celebrate, too happy to collapse in bed, and eventually too worn out to keep awake any more.

When I woke up the next day, I felt that I had been given a new life, a new opportunity, with my empire intact albeit reduced in size, with the possibility that markets might slowly improve beyond the worst we had faced.

After the completion of Chapter 11 proceedings, emerging with a sadly reduced fleet of ships, my focus was on rebuilding the fleet and increasing its numbers as soon as possible, so that we would not be marginalised in the industry. We studied the market and found two areas in which we could invest and grow – we could either increase our reefer fleet or re-enter the bulk cargo sector which was expanding quickly, given China's growing raw material import requirements. Having studied both segments, the thought of becoming the owner of a significant fleet became more and more appealing as did the idea of regaining our status amongst our peers. The industry had written us off. We returned to London revitalised. The industry was astonished. Our reputation started to recover. So, in 2004, we acquired another reefer ship – *Amer Kailash* and in 2005, two more – *Badrinath* and *Kedrnath*.

In hindsight, this was probably a miscalculation on my part for, in my eagerness to regain my world-wide standing in reefer shipping, I had made a compromise and lost out on the more lucrative bulk carrier business, which boomed shortly after we had invested in our reefers. We needed the funds and, rather than going after what we really needed, I had valued and pursued industry status over profitable business.

Towards the end of 2004, we also realised the great opportunities and possibilities in container shipping. This time, I did not miss the opportunity and, at the appropriate time, we acquired two container ships from German owners – *La Bourdonnais* and *Pride of Delhi*. Within five months, China's strategy of flooding western markets with cheaply manufactured goods created an upswing in the container market and created terrific demand for container ships; both of ours were chartered to a prominent German container company and to a French firm. *La Bourdonnais* was scheduled to be renamed *Pride of Mumbai* but, before that could happen, we received an offer for both our newly acquired containers at a premium price – we gave in and sold both, doubling their value in less than seven months.

Now flush with funds. We decided to buy two modern Aframax tankers – *Bareilly* and *Kanpur* – and chartered them to a subsidiary of Glencore of Switzerland for a five year period.

> It takes a lot of courage to show your dreams to someone else.
> Erma Bombeck

In 2004, I found another opportunity while musing on a beach in Goa, at the wedding of my colleague Captain D'Souza's daughter. A thought surfaced in my mind... could Goa, known as the Venice of India, be to the Lakshadweep Islands what Florida was to the Caribbean Islands? The idea grew and grew and, taking to heart the lesson learned early in life about making my dreams a reality, I spoke to Jim Davis, a former P&O man who had joined Foresight as a non-Executive Director in January 2002, who had a great deal of expertise in cruise shipping. Everyone else at Foresight thought I was crazy to enter into this venture, having just come out of bankruptcy proceedings. So I slept on it for a little while, but I had got a bee in my bonnet and I knew that this dream too could become a reality.

Later in the same year, I put together a team to visit a few locations in the areas along the west coast of India, where I planned to run the cruises. We set up Ocean Cruises India in Mumbai, with Leslie Royle as CEO. Then we began the job of liaising with the various ministries of the Indian government, to gain permission to run our line. After talks with Renuka Chowdhury (then Minister of State for Tourism), and clearances from the Ministries of Home Affairs, Shipping and Environment, a clearance letter was issued in March 2005. Since my main idea was to take tourists to the untouched, uninhabited and pristine islands of Lakshadweep, the administration of that Union Territory was then approached to gain their support and assistance for the idea and to organise water sports for them. We were under restrictions that a maximum of two hundred people could access the Islands, and that had to be during daylight hours only. Environmental concerns were put to rest by our agreeing to leave no traces of visitors except footprints in the sand. The cruises, each of six, eight or fourteen day duration, would set out from Goa, and end there as well, taking in the islands of Tinnakara, Suheli, Cheriyan and the Perumalpar Sand Banks, as well as Kochi and Trivandrum on the Indian Malabar Coast, and Colombo in Sri Lanka.

A Memorandum of Understanding was signed in December 2005, and Indian Ocean Cruises, Cyprus would run the service. We bought and outfitted a cruise ship – the *Ocean Odyssey* – and ran the cruises for eight months every year, between October and mid-May, until May 2008, ending only because the infrastructure available at the ports was insufficient to properly support such a luxury cruise. I even sent a proposal to the Indian government to aid them in creating a cruise terminal along with a yacht marina in Goa, but this was lost in the labyrinths of bureaucracy, and remains lost to date, even though we offered to finance it all ourselves.

Fortunately for us, our hospitality ventures had been prospering in the meantime, with new branches of *The Tandoor* opening in Chengdu in 1999 and in Beijing in 2002. Another restaurant, serving South-East Asian cuisine – *The Spice Market* – opened in Shanghai in May 2000. A few years later in June 2004, we reversed the formula and opened *The Chinese* in New Delhi, India, serving authentic Chinese cuisine in an upmarket ambience. *The Tandoor* opened a fourth branch in Guangzhou in July 2008. Then we closed *The Spice Market* in 2009, but only because the property in which it was located had its usage regulations changed to residential rather than commercial.

> We make a living by what we get, but we
> make a life by what we give.
> Winston Churchill

In the meantime, the institute I had set up in Kanpur, AMTA, was looking into the possibility of entering the offshore training sector, where the demand for a course was growing. In March 2007, I sent Captain Bhanti onto our own rig, *Foresight Driller V* which was in Iranian waters, to design a simple course for beginners. The five day

Rig Familiarization Course for Beginners was started at AMTA in June 2008 and has been a resounding success. Very soon AMTA will also start training second mate candidates (navigational officers) for our merchant staff; once that comes through, it will be a full year's daily training schedule for AMTA. I am sure that institute will continue to achieve many more milestones in the forthcoming years.

Our success with GTFC and The Shoe Club Ltd in the shoe components and international supply chain management operations in the early half of the decade brought us to the notice of a few prominent UK shoe retailers. One in particular, the Pavers family from Yorkshire (Pavers UK is the second highest shoe retailer in the UK after Clarks), approached us with a proposition. Their market in the UK was becoming saturated, and they saw greater potential for growth in China and India. China was too competitive and so they decided to enter the Indian market. Their Chairperson, Catherine Pavers, had made it a condition of the expansion plan that they partner with Foresight, and no-one else.

So, in the spring of 2007, I appointed my son-in-law Utsav, the man behind both GTFC and the Shoe Club Limited, to develop a project – Foresight Smart Ventures – focused on India's dynamic growth opportunities. In March 2010, Pavers Foresight Smart Ventures had already established a presence at over eighty retail outlets in all the major metropolises and state capitals of India. The expansion process is ongoing. Our goal for the retail sector is to increase the turnover of this profit centre to one hundred million US dollars by 2014.

* * *

The Foresight Group of Companies, at the start of 2010, has an asset base of over five hundred million US dollars, with market borrowings of less than 40%. Annual turnover is over 15%. The Group has an office each in the UK (London), Cyprus (Nicosia), UAE (Dubai) and Iran (Tehran), and five offices each in China (Shanghai and Beijing) and India (Delhi, Mumbai and Chennai acting as main hubs). The Group has more than one thousand two hundred employees worldwide, comprising over fifty nationalities. The Group's core competencies are shipping, oil drilling and exploration, hospitality and shoe retail.

Over a turbulent decade, we had experienced failure, recovery, mistakes and remedies. Out of our failures came our solutions and, from the near loss of all we had worked for, we rebuilt and grew again, and prospered.

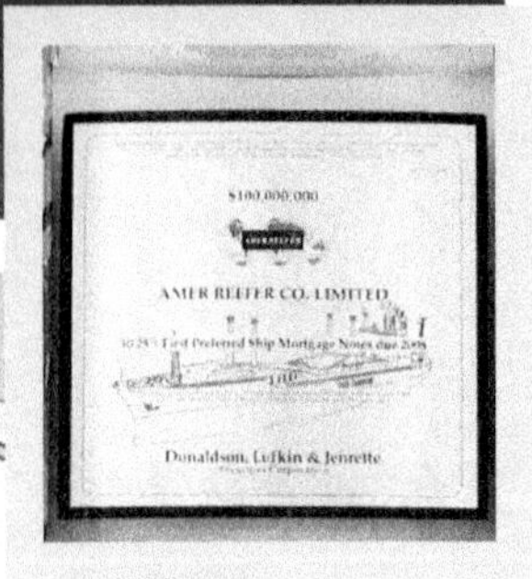

The roadshow: during the hunt for investors in the USA in 1997-98, (clockwise from below left) fast asleep from exhaustion in the plane; the 100 million dollar plaque; recording the successfull conclusion of the bond; getting on the flight to the next meeting; G. Venkat, Mike Revell and Anil Deshpande are ready for the next leg of the journey; DLJ staff Charles Benson and Alice Kang can't stand the pace in the limo, but I win through this time

Facing page above: The port at Nicosia, Cyprus

Below: Wall Street, New York

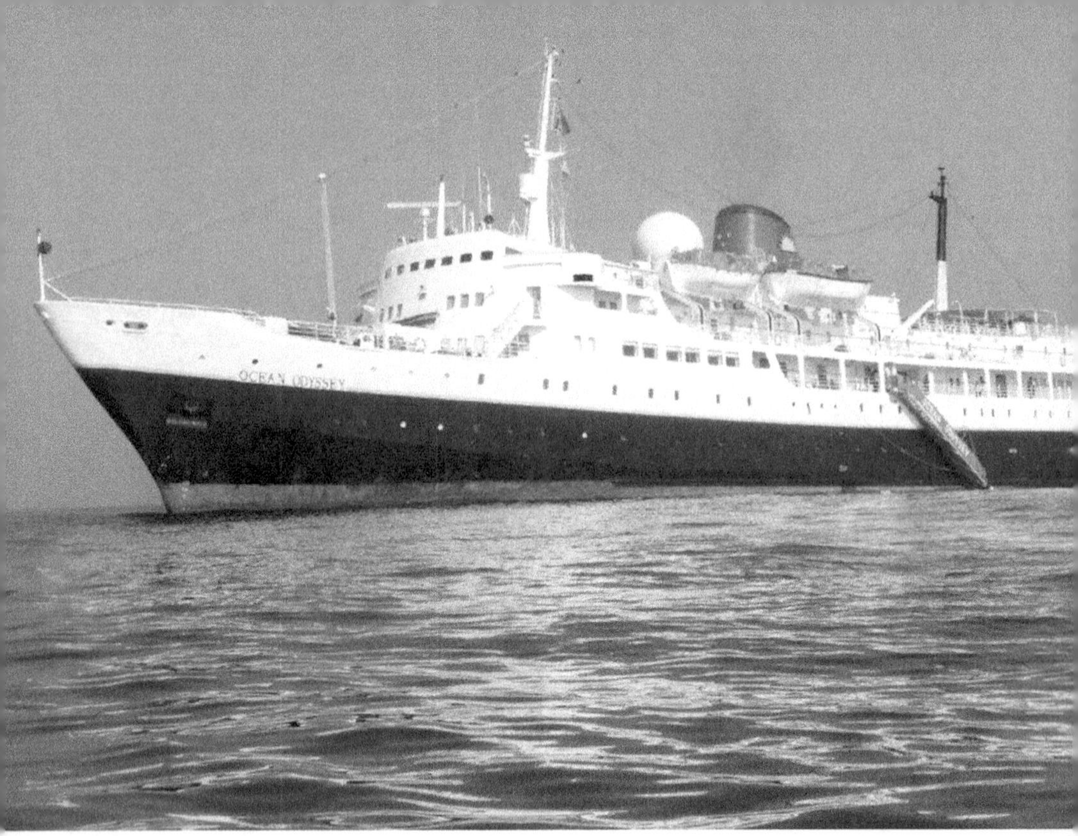
OCEAN ODYSSEY

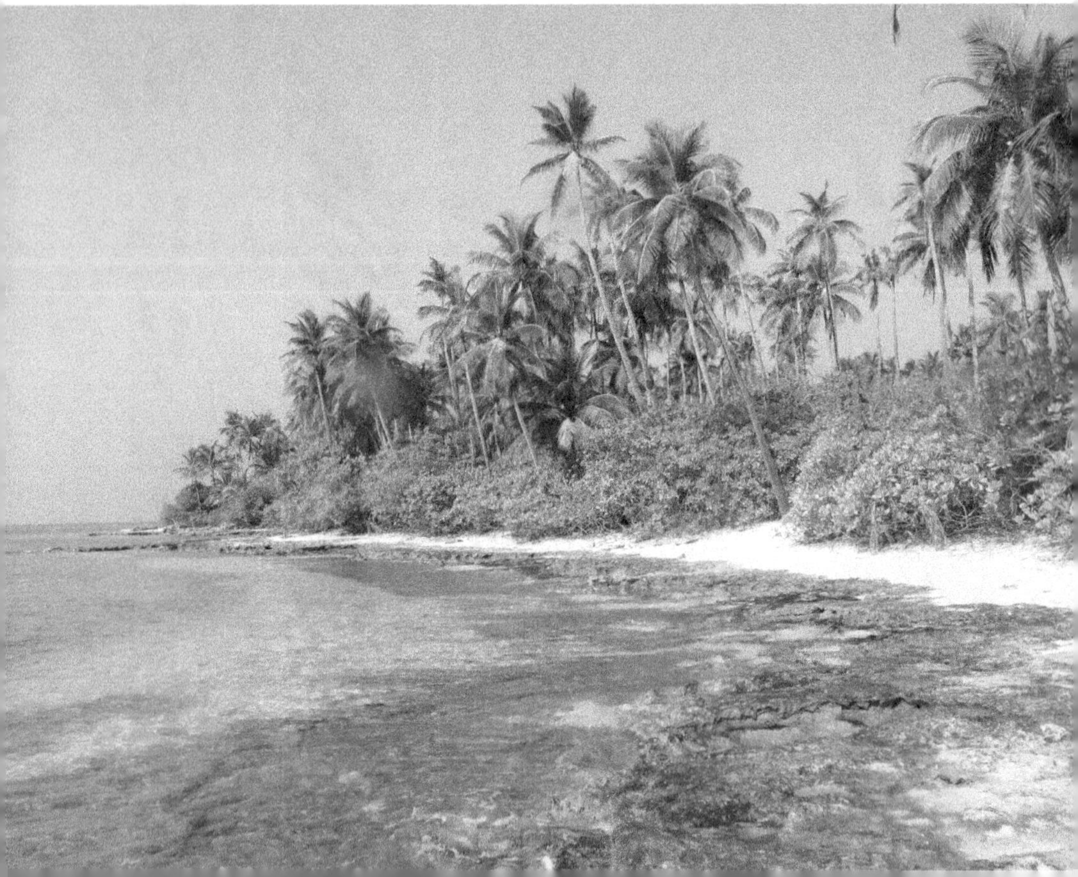

Our hospitality ventures: **Above:** With Mr Sha Lin, of the Shanghai Municipal People's Congress at the opening of *The Spice Market* in Shanghai **Centre:** the Chinese in Delhi, and two of the Tandoor restaurants in China

Facing page: Indian Ocean cruises took passengers on the *Ocean Odyssey* to the beautiful Lakshwadeep Islands of India

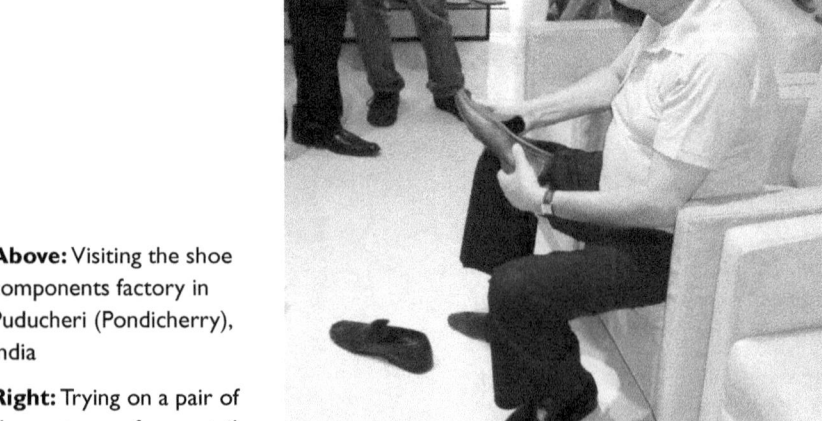

Above: Visiting the shoe components factory in Puducheri (Pondicherry), India

Right: Trying on a pair of shoes at one of our retail outlets

Life Lesson Ten

Regrets and failures are to be learned from, never to be moaned about or repeated. Each day is a new day and a new opportunity to apply the lessons they taught you and to succeed in the new venture.

ENJOY YOUR JOURNEY

Having harvested all the knowledge and wisdom we can from our mistakes and failures, we should put them behind us and go ahead, for vain regretting interferes with the flow of power into our own personalities.

Edith Johnson

Every one of us has failed at something, or regrets some event in our lives — some of us even more than others. A few of those issues we have forgotten; others could still be eating away at us like a disease. Neither failure nor regret can be changed or erased from our past lives, but we can choose to learn from them and to move ahead without any extra baggage. Your regrets can become a millstone upon your shoulders and interfere with every part of your present and future life and degrade your motivation to a debilitating extent. They can cause unhappiness, jealousy and envy, and other dangerous feelings which can only be detrimental to your goal in life. Why carry around your disappointments, missed opportunities and failures, focusing on what could or would have been, and using the words 'If only...'? It is useless to reiterate these words, because you cannot change what has happened. But you CAN and SHOULD change the future by learning all that you can from your failures and regrets. If you are constantly focusing on what you did or didn't do, when will you have time to see what lies ahead? Don't hold on to your past to the detriment of your future. It takes a great deal of courage and objectivity to move on. There is always something better ahead and you will not see it if you keep looking over your shoulder at the past. It is never too late. Remember that encumbering yourself with 'what ifs' will not bring those opportunities back to you. Always focus on what you should have, could have, and WILL have from now on.

The first lesson you must learn as you embark on the path to success is that, though you want to achieve your goals in life, that path is not strewn with rose petals. Life is a hard taskmaster, and you will have to struggle before you reach the top. How soon you reach the pinnacle of success depends upon how much you WANT to achieve your goal. If people tell you they achieved true success without much effort or without going through any hassles, be sure that it is untrue – there is no easy path to success. Hard work, trials and tribulations are all an integral part of it. It is only in fairy tales and perhaps in the lives of the kings and queens of old that life was served up on a silver platter, and even today the Royals also have as tough a life to live as anyone else, though some have greater resources. Your own efforts are paramount, and that is what life and fate will demand of you as a price for success, just as you will doubtless face failure and have regrets along the way.

If you were to ask me today what are my regrets, I would have a tough time defining them clearly, but there have been failures and some causes for regret in my life, the path of which has not always been strewn with rose petals – thorns have pricked my feet many a time. Most of all, I feel that I have usually failed when I let my emotions rule my actions – with the exception of my dealings with the fairer sex, where respecting the emotions and letting your heart lead you rather than your mind is (in most cases) paramount.

Live out of your imagination, not your history.
Stephen Covey

Not only now, but even in the earliest stages of my life, difficulties or humiliations that I faced and situations in which I felt that I had not fared well cropped up fairly often. However, I am fortunate that, perhaps because of some quirk of my upbringing or in my inherent nature, I am able to forget about the adversities I have faced and move on. I have learned from each of these adverse experiences and extracted the lessons to be learnt. So, today, I can say that I *no longer have any regrets*. Now, looking back at a life in which I have achieved a measure of success, I know that it is a God-given boon that I have a mind that does not dwell upon and waste my time upon failures and regrets – I thank my stars that I am able to focus on the positive aspects of my efforts and achievements. Nonetheless, there are still a few incidents that I think of as failures, or adverse situations that I faced, and that I have mixed feelings and regrets about.

> *When one door closes, another door opens; but we often look so*
> *long and so regretfully upon the closed door that we do not see*
> *the ones which open for us.*
> Alexander Graham Bell

The first of the thorns in my life-path was the death of my father when I was only ten years old. He was a great hero to me, and I learnt so much from him in my youth. It was the support of my family that kept me going then, as well as the lessons I had learnt from him about not being regretful about anything. It was he who taught me the game of chess, which I later applied to the game of life, and so this adversity was turned to positivity, and has enhanced my life ever since.

My rustication from DMET in my second year and then my consequent failure to be awarded the President's Gold Medal was a significant cause for regret. I was only able to remain positive by reminding myself that I had done well in all but that one facet, and it served as a constant reminder that mistakes must be paid for, they never just slide gently into the background. You always learn from your mistakes and the fiscal, material or emotional price you paid for them.

> *Fix your eyes forward on what you can do,*
> *not back on what you cannot change.*
> Tom Clancy

In anyone's success, there are always those envious of achievements, and my experiences in this regard have been quite stressful. The earliest one that I can recall came in the early years of my career, when climbing the hierarchical ladder was important to me, since it was the most accessible form of success that I could perceive. My eagerness to achieve resulted in my working extremely hard with never a day of leave, and I was still only twenty-seven years old when I got my Chief Engineer's licence. I sometimes regret having done so because the fact that I had achieved this when I was still so young was an obstacle ever afterwards, through my career with SCI, where seniority, age and rank mattered a great deal. My wife Manju was allowed to accompany me on the bulk carrier Nalanda, despite my lack of the requisite one year's service as Chief Engineer, which prejudiced the Captain, who assumed my youthful promotion was due to head office influence and not hard work or merit.

That led to an adverse relationship throughout his tenure, and made my job as Chief Engineer extremely difficult. My age and my pro-activeness, as well as my outspokenness at the Mumbai Head Office of SCI are also cause for occasional twinges of regret. Once again, it was envy that pushed me into the 'dead-end' section of SCI, and put me in charge of the dredgers. Selected as the second-in-command of the team when we were deputed to Iran was yet another 'issue' for my colleagues at SCI. My age and my lack of seniority were constant obstacles to my competence and my achievements.

It was the same two factors – youth and initiaitive – that led to the next event that troubles me.

I had helped the first Managing Director of Irano Hind achieve his ambitions, by making the company commercially and profitably operational, with the tacit understanding that I would take over when he moved on. Then I was overlooked for that promotion, and Mr L.M.S. Rajawar was next in line – leaving me to suffer regret and endure another three years of watching someone else in the position I felt capable of handling. Rather than run the risk of a recurrence, I switched tactics to so impress the Iranian Chairman, that I followed him into the Managing Director's seat. Had I not done so, the 'seniority and age' issue would have done me in yet again!

I would rather regret some of my failures in life than to live my life failing to forget my regrets.

Greg Ryan

Actual failure was also a fairly regular feature of my professional life – one can hardly be a success one hundred percent of the time! I experienced more of this in my entrepreneurial days than in service with SCI. We tried a great many things before the Iran-Iraq war contract gave us our big break into the market, and set us on the path to success. The next major hiccough was the loss of *Foresight Driller II,* which had to be sold at a massive loss, when a contract with the Oil and Natural Gas Corporation (ONGC) of India fell through – because we were not an India-based company. Next, the Chapter Eleven proceedings in the USA were an extremely rough patch, so much so, it is painful to recall. After that was resolved, and the Company was nursed back to health, I took an truly emotional decision to acquire three reefers rather than re-enter the bulk carrier market, and that was a mistake. My last failure was the decision to run a cruise service in India, and I deeply regret not delving further into it, for I should surely have realised that the cost of that liner would be far more than she could pull in.

All in all, it has been a life of ups and downs, but it has never been boring. All the tough times, the happiness, the struggles and the successes have added up, to provide me with a life rich and full of memories, and wonderful people to relive them with. I hope, at the end, when you have achieved your goal, you can say the same and more. Then, I would feel that my efforts to express myself in this memoir have benefited you. That is the greatest happiness a human being can feel – money and fame have their place, but cannot replace the happiness of the soul. As we grow, we all reach for that ultimate 'inner happiness'.

So much for mistakes and failures. Every one of these has stimulated a pro-active response, determined action, and a positive outcome. There really is no room for real regret.

Above left: Being presented with an Honorary CBE by UK Shipping Minister Stephen Ladyman on behalf of Queen Elizabeth II

Right: Manju and I prepare for a City Livery function shortly after I received the CBE – the first time I was privileged to wear it

Left and Below: My fruit table at the annual Winter Barbeque is famous, and each year, I create a new setting

On one of my frequent visits to AMTA, I received further recognition of my CBE, here in December 2006

Above: My son Saurabh, his wife Neha and their children

Below: My daughter Manjari, her husband Utsav Seth and their children

Above: Manju and I at the Millennium Dinner, with Baroness Margaret Thatcher, in 2001

Below: Manju and I meet Prince Philip (Photograph © John R. Rifkin)

Epilogue

Know when it's time to relax.

IT'S NOT JUST ABOUT MONEY

To be able to fill leisure intelligently is the last product of civilization, and at present very few people have reached this level.

Bertrand Russell

However busy you are, keep a balance in your affairs. Your family is your first refuge and support, and where you can relax at the end of each busy day. Your family gives you the solace you need during rare breaks from a busy life.

The ability to switch off is absolutely essential, I never met a successful man who also enjoyed his success, who had no time to relax, for the truly successful man makes the time to relax. It's part of the plan, the grand scheme, the ultimate achievement, because it lends a certain balance to life.

It may be inherent within you, or more likely, you may have to acquire it. To do so, look at your skills, your resources, your interests. There are always other things we might have liked to do which we set aside in the pursuit of achievement. Every successful entrepreneur should find ways of enjoying time outside work.

The best way for the best and busiest, within their life plan, is to try to make a difference outside business, beyond the demands of the career. There are always areas where your knowledge, experience and ability can be harnessed, whether in the trade bodies of your industry, the voluntary and charitable sectors, or even in simple leisure pursuits.

The satisfaction of helping those in need, lending your mind to education, serving a noble cause, or just mucking about in boats or gardens, or with collectibles or classic cars, or whatever takes your fancy, refreshes the mind, relieves the pressure, recoups the spirit and gives thanks to the God who gave you your gifts. Family and work, with rest and play, make for a truly balanced life.

For a professional with no capital, success is rarely a viable proposition in today's capital intensive industry. Nor is diversification easy. Once success is within reach, it provides another leg to stand on. Most industries are cyclical in nature and, if you choose an industry which is anti-cyclical in relation to your main interests, then you have a better chance of survival, even in times of market depression. The Foresight group of companies has tried to do the same. By God's grace we reached the twenty-five year mark in September 2009. Having begun as a young lad from Kanpur with no claim to fame, I am now one of the most eminent Indians in international shipping.

My lessons in life continue, and I learnt the most recent one in 2006, when I found myself in hospital undergoing a heart bypass. My body was telling me to slow down and take it easy. And yet, it is not simple for a man like me, who has been active and decisive all his life, to simply relax. It has been my dream since I started Foresight Limited that, if my venture was successful, it should continue to prosper and eventually achieve its centenary at the very least. In addition, I was never in it for the monetary success – having a huge bank balance does not excite me. The success of each venture does. As they say, it's how you make the journey that counts.

I believe my success was possible because I began with nothing and no expectations – only ambition. Both my children are now well settled and are part of the Group. There is nothing more that I could wish for, except for them to take my hard work and dreams forward. In 2008, I handed over the post of Chief Executive Officer, to Anil Deshpande, who has been with the Foresight Group for over twenty years, as Managing Director of the Shipping Division. He joined us in 1987, prior to which he had been with me in Iran during my stint with Irano Hind Shipping. I retain the post of Executive Chairman, in which I want to continue until the age of seventy-five at the very least – after that I shall see.

Also in 2006, I was awarded an honorary CBE (Commander of the Order of the British Empire), for my services to international shipping – on the fiftieth anniversary of the coronation of Queen Elizabeth II. I am a member of numerous institutes and associations, and of the Little

Ship Club on the banks of the Thames, where I entertain guests from time to time. I am a director of the Commonwealth Business Council and am a Freeman of the City of London, where I am also a Liveryman of the Worshipful Company of Shipwrights, an ancient City guild and also of the Company of World Traders. I travel regularly to speak at international conferences more than six times a year and am a visiting lecturer at the Academy of Transport in Cambridge, co-Chairman of Europe and India Chambers of Commerce and the India Development Trust.

My wife and I live in London in a Victorian house, built in 1897, which is simple, beautiful and elegant. Both my wife and I still hold Indian passports and have no intention of transferring citizenship, though the authorities hold out lures every now and again. Retaining my Indian citizenship is sacrosanct for both my wife and I. Since Anil took over as the CEO of the Foresight Group, I begin my day (when I am at home in London) with a five kilometre walk and, after brunch at noon, go to my offices in the City, and work till half past eight, when I return home and do a little yoga, followed by a glass of my favourite malt whisky! This is followed by dinner, and I like to have a relaxing massage before I retire to bed.

My favourite pastime is pottering about the garden – I am a keen gardener and like to work with my own hands, for the engineer in me makes that satisfying. I maintain what I like to believe is one of the most beautiful gardens in my neighbourhood. I hold an annual Winter Barbecue on the third Friday evening of the New Year, that has become a landmark of the maritime calendar. Over five hundred guests fly in from all over the world.

I have always been supported by strong women, who have invariably kept me out of trouble. As I have already made clear, I was lucky enough to have a mother who offered me nuggets of wisdom that have helped me all my life. Throughout, my mother Amer Devi Mehrotra's advice has replayed itself in my mind. Other strong women in my life include my wife Manju, a pillar of strength and Claire Horsley who, as my first employee, did not let me make 'quick money' in the early days, and helped me to sustain the Company in the long term. Finally,

Philippa Wright, who joined me as my personal secretary cum office manager, quickly rose to the position of Executive Director of Legal, Administration and Public Relations of Foresight Limited. All of strong character, these four women have sustained me, and ensure that I remain on the straight and narrow in all my business, even though that needs great perseverance on their parts!

This memoir has been written primarily to impart, if possible, hard-learned life lessons, and I hope that they will be helpful to the younger generation, enabling them to gain some insight from another's experiences, and to apply it to their own ventures and circumstances.

For those of you who have gone through all these pages, I hope you have understood that hard work and perseverance, even in the face of adversity, are essential to achieving success. Earning money should not be the main focus of your efforts; it should be a by-product of your actions.

Not all of my Ten Lessons will work for every one of you, because everyone is unique, and has individual problems but, if you can adopt even six or seven of them and apply them to your life, you will certainly succeed in gaining your object. If you can improve upon them you can aim for the stars and, better still, you will be able to pass on the knowledge that you acquire to the next generation, and thus keep the faith. My friends, I wish you all the best in your life and on the path to success.

God bless.

Manju and I posed for this special portrait to celebrate the new cruise venture, and the picture was hung in the ship's reception salon

Ravi's Ten Steps

The Life Lessons that I have imparted in this book are the essence of my life. I hope that they will inspire you and encourage you to reach for the stars... I also hope that you will achieve each and every one of your dreams.

In this part of this book, I begin with the ten-step achievement programme that I feel is essential for all youngsters to map their path to success and achievement, by whatever standards they measure it. It may be helpful to those, like me, who do not have a mentor and need their own wits to help them succeed. In addition, it can be used as a supplement to help those who do have a mentor to plan their success story. I first spoke of this programme at my old high school, it was then published in booklet form and is reproduced here, amended and updated.

Anything is possible, but it all starts with having a dream and then sticking with it through thick and thin.
Steve Case

The sky is the limit, when your heart is in it. And it's the fire in your belly that fires your progress and achievement.
Ravi

HOW TO ACHIEVE

WHAT YOU PLANNED

TO ACHIEVE IN YOUR LIFE

IN

10 Steps
in
40 Days

Mr.Ravi K Mehrotra CBE

The front cover of the original
booklet promoting the Ten Step
programme in India in 2006 –
the picture was taken from the
cruise brochure

I first spoke of my ten step formula for success at the Neasden Temple Children's School in London, and then at the Amer Maritime Training Academy in Kanpur, in December 2006, to enable the young students there to achieve their ambitions and full potential, by following a simple plan.

You may often discover that what you achieve may not be either what you wanted or what you thought to be your potential. You may know what you want but lack the means to get there.

Or perhaps you have the means to get wherever you want to be but do not know where to go. And sometimes, you may know your destination, the path you must take, and even the vehicle that will take you there, but simply lack the determination, the ambition or the urge to begin the journey.

Here, in my ten-step plan, I will share with you a simple method to find a destination, the path to that goal, and a method of tapping into the reservoir of your own resolve to make this possible. Once you have all these in place, you will find that you have far surpassed what you set out to achieve in the first place. I call this journey a 'fire in the belly'.

Welcome aboard!

I have already narrated in detail my own journey, and I have deduced from my forty-seven-plus years of experience that all it takes are ten simple steps, to enable you to achieve greater things than I have, because you create your own mentor inside your mind.

Before we begin, let me share the Pareto Principle with you. It was named after Vilfredo Pareto, an Italian philosopher, and is also known as the 80/20 theory. Let me explain it simply, by comparing it to how a shepherd manages more than a hundred goats when he takes them to pasture. He maintains a lead goat and it is usually eighty percent of the goats who follow that lead goat. His task is then to control only the remaining twenty percent.

What the Pareto Principle implied was that people are like the goats I have just described: eighty percent of us follow the rules society makes for us, and it is the remaining twenty percent who think 'outside the box', and who comprise both positive and negative thinkers.

So, there are three categories of people in our society. Firstly, there are those who are happy to follow what the majority is doing, and they remain contented. Secondly, there are the negative thinkers, who like to break regulations and always end up in trouble. And thirdly, the remainder are the positive thinkers, who attempt to make the best use of the regulations, turning them to their greatest advantage.

It is imperative that you decide in which of these categories you belong:

Average – 80%?

Destructive – about 10%?

Constructive – the remaining top 10%?

For the first two categories, there is no help that I can provide. If you want to be in the third category of the constructive ten percent, then follow the ten steps I have outlined here. Once you have outlined your own ten step path to success, keep them confidential and share them with no-one, because jealousy of another's success is a human emotion that may hinder you on the path to success.

The way to be is to do nothing.

Nathaniel Howe

"The finest leaders I have dealt with possess three qualities above all else: skill a as listener, skill as a delegator and skill as a motivator. These traits require a degree of modesty scarce among those ambitious enough to clamber to the top. ... Such thrusting figures often possess considerable egos and want to maximise personal glory. By contrast, wise bosses know that progress is rarely achieved through noisy triumphs, like imagined events in fiction, but through unflashy, incremental steps that take time and a team effort. This runs counter to the desire for headlines and simplistic answers and our thirst for personalities. The reality is that a consistent five per cent annual growth rate still doubles the size of a company every fourteen years and is likely to create a much sounder enterprise than a more frantic display."

— Luke Johnson

THE 10 STEP PROGRAM

Self-doubt is the little voice in your head
saying 'You Can Do It!' and the big voice saying
'I Wish You Would'...listen to the little voice.

Sean O'Donnell

STEP ONE

Take a sheet of paper and write down at least six hobbies or interests in which you have a level of proficiency and in which you would like to indulge. For the next two days, continue your other normal routine, and just mull over each of the six items whenever you have the time. Consider how and why and to what level you like these activities. Consider their pros and cons in relation to you. Also consider how society will react to your pursuit of them in the future. You can talk to others about their positive and negative effects both now and in the next ten years. But do not tell them why you are discussing such things.

NOTES

_____

_____

_____

_____

_____

_____

_____

_____

_____

_____

_____

_____

_____

_____

STEP TWO

After the two days of thought, you are now ready to put these six items in the order of your preference. Then select the top three and discard the remaining three. Use the next three days to revisit each of the three remaining areas of your interest, and see how you would like it if you were to succeed at any of them. I will disclose later why I want you to sleep with only one career choice or hobby on your mind each night. Go to sleep at night with one of the items on your list in your mind. When you wake up, list your thoughts about that particular career choice. Do this for the next t wo nights with the other two items on your list. At the end of the three days, put these three items in your revised order of preference. Then select the top two careers and discard the third one.

NOTES

_____
_____
_____
_____
_____
_____
_____
_____
_____
_____
_____
_____
_____

STEP THREE

At this stage you have selected two options for your career and now your agony of indecision is almost over. Congratulations, you have completed a huge step! The third step is that you need to turn over the job of selecting a career to a permanent twenty-four hour live-in genie who serves you like a steadfast servant, provided to you by God – your subconscious mind. It is now your subconscious mind that will do the final selection for you. Putting the subconscious mind to work is an important step. Many people do not achieve their full potential because their subconscious mind does not support their physical efforts.

Your job is now to increase your awareness of your inner being, your subconscious mind. Once you accept your own subconscious mind, you need to throw it a challenge and tell it to select the career that will become your destiny. If you activate this initial introspection, your subconscious mind will never make you feel guilty about not having consulted it, and you will not look back with regrets. Having placed the onus of the choice on your subconscious mind, it will become more aware of its responsibilities. You have to be very careful here, as most people fail because they do not seek the support and companionship of their subconscious mind in their efforts. Here I will repeat that your subconscious mind has to support your physical efforts – in the same way that sportsmen and scientists use mind and body together to win Olympic medals and Nobel prizes.

During the next two days you will realise that you are dreaming at night of what must select as your career for the next ten years. Your subconscious mind will bring out, subtly, which one of the two careers you have consciously selected is better for you. You are now ready to proceed, and you have your final choice of career. It has taken you only seven days since the beginning of this exercise. What you have accomplished is enormous. And in just seven days! I have watched people struggle for years to finally make the right career choice.

NOTES

_____
_____
_____
_____
_____
_____
_____
_____
_____
_____
_____
_____
_____
_____
_____
_____
_____
_____
_____
_____
_____
_____

STEP FOUR

Having discovered the destination (or goal) of life's journey, the next important step is finding the path or map to that destination. How do you get there? Have you ever known anyone who simply decided to run in the Olympics and won a Gold Medal? No. They had to work hard to achieve that medal, and so will you, to reach your goal. Remember though, that unlike others in the race of life, you are already ahead. For one, you have chosen your career path and have no doubts. In addition, you now have two twenty-four hour live-in genies, working together for you – your conscious and subconscious minds. What you now need is a very clear and precise plan to implement so that you and your genies can keep track of it. Always remember, your subconscious mind is your servant, so all pro-active thinking has to be done by your conscious mind.

Remember that your plan should have established norms so that even your servant can follow them. These norms, outlined in clear terms without any ambiguity, should be:

- A starting point outlining your present position

- An ultimate goal to be reached at the end of ten years

- Means – both financial and emotional support from family and well-wishers

- Distractions – try to quantify or recognise possible inner distractions (emotional distractions that take you away from your goal) and outer distractions (jealousy or envy exhibited and acted upon by your rivals and competitors that will keep you from reaching your goal)

- A Time Limit – the time between your starting and finishing points, which is already set at ten years

- Rewards at each step for achieving goals along the path to your ultimate goal

- Punishments or consequences for non-completion on the way

- Difficulties along the way – how to overcome them

- Imponderables – how to bypass them

- Ultimate recognition of success

Discuss within your mind each of the ten norms which help to make and develop a plan into a precise one, with a high probability of success. Many plans fail because they have not been constructed properly in the first place. All possible scenarios must be explored at the very outset, even making allowances for unforeseen difficulties.

NOTES

STEP FIVE

Once your plan has been prepared in detail, stop working on it and mull over it for three days. Challenge your subconscious mind, and let it look at the plan, pick holes in it and tell you all its reservations about the plan. Because, once you are set on the path to your destination, changing your plan is nearly impossible. There is no going back on it. Don't let your subconscious mind have the opportunity to point a finger at you later on and say 'You did not consult me'! You will be surprised at the dreams and suggestions the subconscious mind can come up with, once it is pushed into use. Now factor these suggestions made by your subconscious into your plan. It is not necessary that all your subconscious mind's suggestions are correct. If they are not, you are free to argue it out with your subconscious mind and point out holes in its plans. Your subconscious mind will appreciate this, because the subconscious also wants you to be as committed to this plan as you want your subconscious to be – that is how it tests your resolve. Also bear in mind, your subconscious mind reciprocates your commitment and resolve. At the end of ten days your plan is ready for adoption. Begin immediately, and do not waver. Celebrate the start of your journey on the path to success, the same way as Indians celebrate the laying of a foundation stone at a project-site.

NOTES

STEP SIX

The sixth step is the most difficult one. Having completed the first five steps, you may feel you can relax because there is ample time – ten years – to achieve your goal. But it is because of this very attitude you rarely see a foundation stone laid in India and built up into a vibrant project. The next million dollar step is figuring out how to ensure that your plan, crafted with such great care, is implemented. How? The issue here is that one is so busy with life's mundane activities that one has no time to see what the plan will gain at the end of ten years. Do you have any ideas? The solution is easy – divide your big plan into smaller more manageable plans, to keep your focus. But it's easier said than done.

NOTES

_____

_____

_____

_____

_____

_____

_____

_____

_____

_____

_____

_____

_____

_____

_____

_____

STEP SEVEN

First, map out how your ten year plan can be converted into ten plans of one year each. In other words, each of your plans builds upon the plan of the previous year, so that, at the end of ten years, you achieve the same goal you planned in Step Five.

Can you do it? Try. Always remember that any plan, whether it is of short or long duration, must be complete. It must have all ten norms itemised in Step Four and, like your ten year plan, each little one year plan must have a starting point and a goal.

It is essential that they are complete in themselves for ease of implementation. The only thing you have to ensure is that the direction of each one yearly plan leads to the achievement of your ultimate goal. Your yearly plans are like the pieces of a jigsaw puzzle. As individual pieces, they may not make much sense. But together, they form a beautiful picture. That beautiful picture is your ten-year plan that you created in Step Five.

You should take two days to craft each plan. In all, twenty days for ten plans. So at the end of thirty days since beginning this ten step programme, you will have your ten one-year plans.

You must take great care in moulding these sub-plans. Your plan for the first year should be perfect and steadfast. But your plans from year two to ten must make provisions to incorporate the experiences, and the knowledge, that come from the mistakes you will have made in the implementation of the first yearly plan. But remember, the final goal should not be altered at any cost. The only freedom you should allow yourself is that of the finer details of implementation, because they are the only ones that will keep changing because of changing circumstances around you.

No matter what, the new plan should always be ready by the eleventh month of the current plan, so that the new plan is implemented by the deadline you have set for yourself.

NOTES

_____

_____

_____

_____

_____

_____

_____

_____

_____

_____

_____

_____

_____

_____

_____

_____

_____

_____

_____

_____

_____

STEP EIGHT

At the end of thirty days you will have your detailed first year plan, with a further nine yearly plans outlined. It will be good to make provisions for those among your acquaintances who would support you and be willing to lend a helping hand. Once again, a year comprising three hundred and sixty-five days is too elongated a period for you and for your subconscious mind to focus upon. There is a possibility of your losing focus and becoming lax. Ideally, each yearly plan should be broken down into daily tasks. This may seem like a tedious task, so you will find yourself inventing ways to dodge doing this. If you are diverted at this point, all this planning will be for naught, and you will fail.

So then, what do we do to make it succeed? There are only two alternatives – one is a weekly plan and the other monthly. I suggest a monthly plan so that, if you are lagging behind in any given month, you can catch up in the next month – break your first year's plan into twelve monthly sub-plans. In the eleventh month of each year, you must plan to undertake the task of dividing the next year into twelve sub-plans, on the basis of your progress at that point. Converting your yearly plan into twelve steps should not take more than seven days. At the end of the thirty-seventh day, you should be ready to implement your vision of 'What (or where) do I want to be in ten years?' For the next three days, relax and sleep on it. Don't forget to remind yourself and your subconscious mind each day that, after this period, you cannot alter your plan. You are both irretrievably committed to it.

NOTES

_____

_____

STEP NINE

Your forty days are now over. At the end of the fortieth day, when you get up, do not worry. Your subconscious mind will be constantly exhorting you to implement the first months of your first year's plan. You are now on your way to implementing your Dream Vision and Goal, whatever it is that you decided you want to be at the end of ten years. You are now a changed person. You are not alone. You have your subconscious mind with you each step of the way. Your self-confidence is enhanced. You are ready to brave the world.

NOTES

STEP TEN

Always remember that, although your subconscious mind is your genie to serve you, it is also a merciless tyrant. It has an elephantine memory. It never ever forgets what you have asked it to commit to. It will keep popping up incessant reminders from which you cannot escape. This means you must follow your plan ruthlessly. Having done that, the next important step is to reward yourself every month when you complete your monthly goals. Be sure to decide in advance what the reward will be for each monthly and yearly completion of your sub-plans. Finally, decide in advance what you want to give yourself when you achieve your ten year goal. These awards are very important for the subconscious mind, because that way it can remind you each time that it is the subconscious mind that has got you that award. Always be grateful to it! The subconscious mind is your genie given by God, but it will remind you always that your success is because of and not in spite of it.

NOTES

At the end of this particular journey in which I have helped you plan your own journey, what award will you give me, for having given you in simple words what I have practised and perfected in the last forty-seven years? My reward shall simply be immense pleasure when I discover that at least a few of you have achieved more than I have managed to achieve in my life – especially if you begin with just dreams and an empty pocket as I did. Thank you my friends, and good luck.

That some achieve great success, is proof to all that others can achieve it as well.

Abraham Lincoln

Testimonials

SHEILA DIKSHIT
CHIEF MINISTER

सत्यमेव जयते

GOVT. OF NATIONAL CAPITAL TERRITORY OF DELHI
DELHI SECRETARIAT, I.P. ESTATE
NEWDELHH10113
PHONE: 23392020, 23392030
FAX: 23392111
D.O.NO.:
Dated:

FOREWORD

I am pleased to learn that book titled **"What's in it for YOU"** is being published by Shri Ravi Kumar Mehrotra. It gives me pleasure to learn that all proceeds from the sale of this book will be donated to Non-Profit-Institution established by the writer.

The book carries the story of the writer's journey from a marine engineering student to a multibillion dollar entrepreneur. Through this book a lot could be learnt by the youngsters who aspire to become successful in their life.

The writer has given an account of his efforts and initiatives while underlining the need of a balanced approach and risk and time management which, in fact, remain crucial throughout the life. The book enunciates the principle to find right track to move further in the direction towards success. It contains all that is needed to face the challenges in this fast changing world where quest of carrier enrichment is becoming more and more significant. I am sure that this book will be useful to one & all.

My best wishes for successful publication of the book.

Sheila Dikshit

(SHEILA DIKSHIT)
CHIEF MINISTER, DELHI

The answer to Ravi's question "What is in it for you ?" is a fascinating book full of interest, humour and intriguing philosophy which is embodied in his ten lessons from life which helped him succeed.

It gets off to a great start with an exceptionally good foreword by Sir Mark Tully who said that he learned most from the Ravi's ten lessons from life the idea of "positive discontentment" meaning "remain positive but discontented with what you achieve, it will keep you aiming even higher and keep the fire burning in your belly"

The text is full of inspiring quotes on all aspects of life and his Ravi Formula have obviously proved to be very effective particularly his emphasis right at the start that his family was the bedrock of everything he did. Although he has worked harder than most men he stresses that work should only be one part of life and has to be balanced with other equally important activities. He advocates simple but unusual advice such as avoid signing cheques yourself so that you don't look at the money as being your own. Work for progress and achievements rather than monetary gain as wealth is a bonus but not your goal.

Ravi has been honest about his own feelings of fear and disappointment but they never seemed to get him down. He always bounced back with renewed vigour. On one occasion his entry into a particular country was barred so gets gets a lift in a fishing vessel. When the engine breaks down it is Ravi that repairs it then and there.

He took risks but was never reckless in building up his immensely successful commercial enterterprises. Perhaps one of the most important factors in his outstanding success was his concern for the individual. He treated his employees as members of his company. His philosophy was to be forgiving for we all make mistakes. Ravi is a remarkable man and this is a truly fascinating book.

Lord Ian McColl of Dulwich, CBE
Conservative member of the House of Lords, UK

Ravi Mehrotra is among the most fascinating practitioners of shipping in his generation. From humble beginnings, he became a renowned tanker owner, famous for canny investments and whose every move was tracked by the industry. He was an early internationalist, who understood the changing political and economic scenarios in the Middle East and East Asia, and is unique in his ability to straddle seemingly opposing cultures and develop successful business strategies in challenging environments. He is one of the founders of modern Iranian shipping, and was an early mover in China. A man of resourcefulness and good will, he has devoted time and effort to improve the lives of seafarers and maritime education in India and Iran.

In his book, What's in it for You, Mr Mehrotra offers far more than a business memoir. While the book is ideal for readers who want to find out about the Mehrotra legacy, it also presents a powerful and useful introduction to a career in shipping.

But is more than this again. What's in it for You is an examination of the relation between successful action and a spiritual search for moral, reasonable action in the difficult, sometimes savage arena of global business. Mr Mehrotra writes concisely, entertains as well as instructs and demonstrates a flair for story-telling. As such, What's in it for You can be recommended as a must-read for youthful aspirants of all ages who are seeking a step-by-step advance in business with a view to retaining a full and rich inner life.

Mr Tom Leander,
Editor-in-Chief Asia of the Lloyd's List
(global shipping newspaper).

"What's in it for you" with ten lessons of life, is worth reading for anyone who has great ambitions, high values for hard work, wishes to be a lifetime achiever, while also making his or her dream come true. The work portrays a fascinating experience of marine life from the days of a cadet to the days of corporate and then building on a 500 million dollars asset the "Foresight Group".

The autobiography is an astonishing work of self understanding and revelation of a peerless and provocative sensibility. Describing his childhood in Kanpur, his days of learning at DMET, Calcutta and telling a story of attaining success from his own fiercely independent point of view - Mehrotra fashions a book of deep conviction, charm and intimacy, which will be a stepping block for all the new generations.

His treatment of his childhood, his disillusionment when his father passed away and the gratitude to his mother for giving the valuable lessons of life, which he cherishes and values even today, is highly factual and coalesces well with every successive triumph he rode from 1963 till this day.

The autobiography of Ravi Kumar Mehrotra is an excellent book and very comprehensive & interesting to read. The author is to be credited for the simplicity with which he has comprehended his entire life, narrating some of the most striking encounters of his career which invokes a feeling of positivity and challenges every reader to take life as an opportunity.

The book turns out to be a wonderful reckoner for a stage-by-stage planning and to outline a path of success, for the 10% bravos in this world, as Ravi terms them, the constructive people, people with positive discontentment.

Taking a closer introspection of the twists and turns in the story, there are as such no new ideas being generated in this book, but it reaffirms the belief by all the great people of the world that success is truly achieved by only those who have to their credit a positive mind-frame, desire to sweat, make the most out of the worst state of affairs, exhibit a will to win and be upbeat about winning from failures too. The book has 10 life lessons and I am amazed at the way he has used his experiences to educate the masses. As with the title "What's in it for you", I find there is a lot in it for you and every reader will come away feeling richer.

I observed that the days spent in Iran was the most crucial in the life of Ravi, when he was stuck in dilemmas of risk, conflicts and several new ventures. His account of that period thus involves a long and a one-on-one account of the several experiences, right from 1975 when the family started with their journey in Iran staying in a villa in Zargendeh, till he winded up from Iran on Sept 4, 1984, when Ravi's inner conscience finally prompted him to venture into his own business with "Foresight Limited" at London. During the most turbulent years, he played a leading role in developing Iranian Shipping Fleet and self sufficiency in import and export of goods considered vital for Iranian economy. Ravi devotes nearly 25 pages of business adventure to this account which portrays the formation of Indo-Iranian joint venture "Irano Hind", the Iranian Revolution and the Iran Iraq war of 1980.

The author has tasted success in almost all the endeavors undertaken in his life, while working for SCI, expanding the Shipping fleet in Iran and the upgrowth success of his own enterprise 'Foresight', except for a very few of the regrets where he had to confront with stormy waters, but then what is a life without risk? I am reminded of the quote of Pierre Corneille "To win without risk is to triumph without glory".

The book seems to strengthen the reader's confidence while looking at the rewarding plans and strategies of Foresight Group Chairman, reviewing investment opportunities and expanding business from shuttle service management to offshore drilling & reefer shipping and adding fleet of tankers, multipurpose ships to the wealth of the Foresight Limited.

Once a sailor and now a UK based Indian entrepreneur Ravi K Mehrotra, passed through the looking glass of fame and honoring his services to the shipping industry, was chosen by Queen Elizabeth II for an honorary Commander of the Most Excellent Order of the British Empire.

It is arresting to look at the photos of early days of Ravi with all the family members to be always reminded of his formula that it is very important to find a balance with the work, recreation and the time you spend with your family. The image of Ravi, at page 82, smoking a pipe reveals his entrepreneurship personality and wonderfully depicts his life lesson that "every challenge is an opportunity, so risk it and win it". The snapshots at the end of each lesson is abundant proof of how this marine engineer ventured into the big world, taking ordeals across the seas, exploring new territories and standing out amongst the extraordinary men and women. Every picture reveals in its own remarkable way his relentless, obsessive drive to expand horizons and move forward in his life.

The book has provided me a strong sense of inspiration, motivation and learning. I am sure, with a little bit of Ravi Kumar Mehrotra inside all of us, We, which includes all the future potential readers, will definitely achieve a lot of excellence.

Reading "What's in it for you", I am left full of admiration and it makes me wonder what Ravi's journey of foresight will achieve next.

(Sudhir Vasudeva)
Chairman, ONGC

I first met Mr Ravi Mehrotra, one late night in 1993, at our common friend Mr Ganapathy's residence in London. I was trying to understand the global shipping sector and had landed up in London. 'Guru', as he was introduced to me, had taken the trouble to drive over, to meet a fresh upstart researcher from IIMA. It was a brief meeting, but he had sensed a possible future, well before I had.

A little later, when along with three other colleagues and with the support of the Vasant Sheth Memorial Foundation, we organised a top management workshop on the shipping sector, Ravi showed up at IIMA, to lend his shoulder to our continuing efforts on the shipping sector. He spent a whole day with us on the deliberations towards designing a management development programme for senior management in the shipping sector. Not only that, but by the end of the day, he had promised a three week all expenses paid internship for four of us to visit his London and Cyprus offices for an indepth exposure to the shipping sector. He also agreed to throw open Foresight for a set of management cases which we could document for use in the management development programme. That was a memorable summer, well spent in Cyprus and UK. Thanks to Guru, there was a lot of learning about the maritime sector. Four cases were documented, used with great value in the programme and subsequently published in the book Shipping Management: Cases and Concepts. Ravi too wrote a piece for the book. He came in as the inaugural speaker for the third offering of the programme, which by then had become a successful offering at IIMA. And then to clinch the relationship further, his son Saurabh came as a participant in the next offering, to become a programme alumni!

We have stayed in touch intermittently, with my doing a few visits to London and he to Ahmedabad. Of course, the visit to Khajuraho for the family wedding was a grand treat. It has indeed been wonderful knowing Ravi.'

Ravi's action orientedness and entrepreneurial abilities stand out. I find his eye for detail, while retaining the big picture really admirable. This comes through in the book in a remarkable manner. A plain speaking autobiography, his painstaking efforts at providing a ten lesson structure to leave a legacy to budding achievers is wonderful. Ravi reaches out to those without mentors, using his life as a case study. For a case study using academic like me in the area of logistics, the book has valuable insights in grit, leadership and risk management. The war years story of limiting risks to the Gulf by positioning a tanker as warehouse is an example of clever and daring acumen. The persevering efforts against the American investors to retain control over his business baby is a lesson in sheer survival in today's unforgiving financial world.

The meticulously apt selection of quotations in his narrative shows the perfectionist instinct in the man. I really enjoyed this. His personality in enjoying the finer aspects of life, be it in being part of an elite professional group or having a 'relaxing' massage is charming. The book is rigorously edited and reads well.

Prof. G Raghuram
Indian Institute of Management, Ahmedabad

Ravi Mehrotra is a remarkable man. His life experience projects a rich tapestry of success achieved through sheer determination and hard work.

The introduction to his book reminds us that this is a work of non-fiction. Those who have known him would not need to be reminded that this is so. He represents truth in its simplest form.

We all look for role models in life. We enjoy the company of opinion formers. Add to this the ingredient of modesty and you have before you the figure of Ravi Mehrotra. He is gentle but decisive. He is passionate about causes he supports. In almost all conversations there is the sprinkling of humour which puts you at ease.

So what is it about Ravi Mehrotra which singles him out from others? How can a person of ethnic background break the mould of disadvantage and discrimination and rise to such heights?

His early career and life experiences that follow throw a remarkable insight in the way he has advanced in life.

A qualification in Marine engineering led him to a career in the shipping industry. So far so good but what makes him different from others.

At the time of India's independence in 1947 there were problems associated with the emergence of a new nation. The migration of Indians to the United Kingdom and to other parts of the world was a direct result of the economic situation prevailing in that country. It would be years before the situation would improve. It is no surprise that this young marine engineer had his sights on a career abroad.

Ravi does not look for simple solutions. It would be tempting to build a career with a gold watch and a reasonable pension at the end of it. Instead Ravi Mehrotra goes for setting up his own shipping company.

It could not have been an easy task because in those early years the relations between Indians and the native Britons were shaped by the colonial encounters and the unequal economic and political power relationship that existed then.

In those early years assumptions were made that Britain was a truly melting pot, that all the many racial, cultural and religious groups would be assimilated into a new whole – a single people with similar ideals, attitudes and values. The process was thought to be automatic inevitable, impersonal and something that would affect future generations.

Unfortunately there was very little realisation that people like Ravi Mehrotra do not allow others to shape their destiny. They do it for themselves backed by years of civilised values and beliefs and culture which are a trademark of Indians all over the world.

Indians to a great extent retained their identities. They were part of the cultural pluralism that had emerged. Never before Britain had seen such pluralism supplemented by the visual identity of the individuals. The shadow of the colonial encounters, the master servant relationship– were no longer the realities of the colonies. They had come to Britain to break that mould.

A considerable emphasis has been made in stereotyping Indians in the UK as a success story. Ravi Mehrotra has never forgotten that his profile was shaped by the economic restructuring and the recession that occurred in the 1980s. In our fast changing world, there is a change in attitude, a new assertiveness. People are better educated and more questioning of authority than ever before and better informed too. Perhaps at the root of all his success, Ravi has never stopped questioning everything he does. He abhors conformity and challenges are never frightening to him.

All this leads us to a remarkable man who demonstrates in his book independence, self-reliance, openness, diversity and pluralism.

It is a "must read" for our up and coming generations.

The Lord Dholakia of Waltham Brooks, OBE PC DL

Thank you so much for your wonderful book. It was a lovely surprise to receive it and although I have only scanned it quickly I look forward to reading it in more depth during the recess.

What I did glean from it though is that you have had an extraordinary life and used special "footsteps" to keep you on a forward-facing path. Your enthusiasm for all you have done and your remarkable achievements are testament to your determined and wise decision making processes – and I commend you wholeheartedly for them. Indeed, they are an inspiration to younger people and may help them to focus on what is important in this life and how best they can achieve their goals.

So thank you Ravi – and I look forward to reading it with more leisure time than I have at present!

I do hope to see you again before too long.

Ever,

Angela (Angie – as all my lot call me!)
Baroness Angela Harris, House of Lords, UK

I personally know Mr Ravi Kumar Mehrotra for decades and I truly consider him as a friend. In his book titled "What's in it for you?" Mr. Mehrotra has shared his true life experiences which helped him gain wisdom to succeed in different and difficult phases of his life.

His exhilarating journey, beginning just as a cadet (Marine Engineer) to becoming a Shipowner, unfolds the true spirit of an unbeaten entrepreneur. His success is of more significance to me as his career originated with the Shipping Corporation of India Ltd.

But what appealed to me the most is the fine balance which Mr Ravi Kumar Mehrotra could achieve in his life between his dedication to career, commitment to the family and being a wonderful human being at the same time. I think this has made him a 'Complete Man', which is a rarity in the present time. And precisely this is the concept of success which he is offering to his readers through his ten 'Life Mantras'.

All in all, it was a great experience going through this book and I would say that "What's in it for you?" definitely contains something valuable which will appeal and inspire all the readers.

Mr. S. Hajara
Chairman & Managing Director
The Shipping Corporation of India Ltd.
Shipping House, Mumbai

Ravi Mehrotra's autobiography is a well-illustrated canter through his life, first as a young man determined to make his mark as a professional marine engineer and then of the second quarter century during which his ambitions to become an independent shipowner were fulfilled. It is amply supported by examples drawn from nearly fifty years associated with the industry, a time for many which is has been turbulent yet which provided some unique opportunities to turn a modest investment into a fortune. Mark Tulley's Foreword shows special insight into Mehrotra's life as he shares with him a great love of the author's beloved homeland of "Mother India". Tulley's reference to If by Rudyard Kipling is a hint of what follows in the main text: the challenges, the failures and the successes of Ravi Mehrotra's career from trainee marine engineer to a captain of the industry, entrepreneur par excellence.

As the narrative takes place in the modern era of shipping, it will have special resonance for the several generations of the shipping industry that have lived through this same time period. Mehrotra, however, goes beyond the autobiographical genre and delivers an insightful "ten-step achievement programme" which provides a template of success for the young recruits making their way in the shipping industry today.

His "true grit" determination is established early when as an interviewee for a trainee placement with the Indian Directorate of Marine Engineering and Training he was confronted with the accusation that he was using his father's reputation to enhance his career – despite the fact that he had been dead nearly nine years by this time. Mehrotra responded boldly by declaring he "did not need anyone's help to succeed". His place was secured and he went on to have an illustrious career with the Shipping Corporation of India, a State-owned enterprise set up after Indian independence.

It was during this period of his life that he was posted to Iran in 1975 to assist in the formation of an Indian/Iranian shipping joint venture, the Irano-Hind Shipping Company. After the Iranian Revolution of 1979 overthrew the Shah, Mehrotra remained in Iran at the personal request of the Ayatollah Khomeini to oversee the development of Irano Hind and later to take responsibility for nationalising the Arya National Shipping Line which became the Islamic Republic of Iran Shipping Line (IRISL).

These early successes during the most challenging of times (the Iran-Iraq War began in September 1980 during his time in Teheran) has stood him in great admiration by not only the Iranians but also many of his contemporaries in the international shipping industry.

Iran was the proving ground for the young and ambitious Mehrotra, and it was soon after that he moved his family to London to try his hand at establishing his own shipping enterprise. In his own words he "did not wish to miss the opportunity... to change from being a professional to being an entrepreneur". Foresight Shipping was born in September 2004 with considerable enthusiasm but not the capital to match. How he turned this bleak position into a solid shipowning enterprise is a conjuring trick to behold and which, unlike the magicians of the Magic Circle, Mehrotra goes on to reveal. Along the way, the old shipping adage of "buy cheap, sell dear" was used to great effect.

It is this second half of the book that I personally found most illuminating as it shed light on a period in shipping which saw many established names disappear for lack of cash. How then did Ravi Mehrotra confront the odds and move his own start-up company to a position of strength? Of particular interest to many will be the story behind the Amer Reefers' High Yield Bond issue. The subsequent collapse of the bond value forced the company to take protective action. Mehrotra's candid explanation of the actions of the players involved and their motivations and objectives is a case study in Junk Bond failures which every student of ship finance should read.

This book has something to give for everyone who reads it. It is also one of the few chances to receive insight into how someone can move from relative obscurity to being a successful and wealthy independent shipowner. Ravi Mehrotra's autobiography is also an historic insight into one of the most turbulent periods in shipping history, and the story of perseverance leading to success. The short personal comments by the author which introduce each chapter can be joined together to reveal what makes a good person and a good manager; in short, what made Ravi Mehrotra.

Dr John M Doviak
Director, Cambridge Academy of Transport, Cambridge

"Ravi is a true ambassador of India's thoughts, traditions and, above all, entrepreneurship. His mantras for the success in life and business are simple, smart and, more importantly, straight from the heart. The book brilliantly brings out Sangam – that he is – of the two worlds – East and West! Read the book for a new dawn, a new awakening in your life !

–Narendra Taneja, Journalist, commentator and thinker

www.ingramcontent.com/pod-product-compliance
Lightning Source LLC
Chambersburg PA
CBHW061507180526
45171CB00001B/71